The Roman Empire vs. America:
How the American Ideal Echoes the Rise and Fall of the Roman Empire

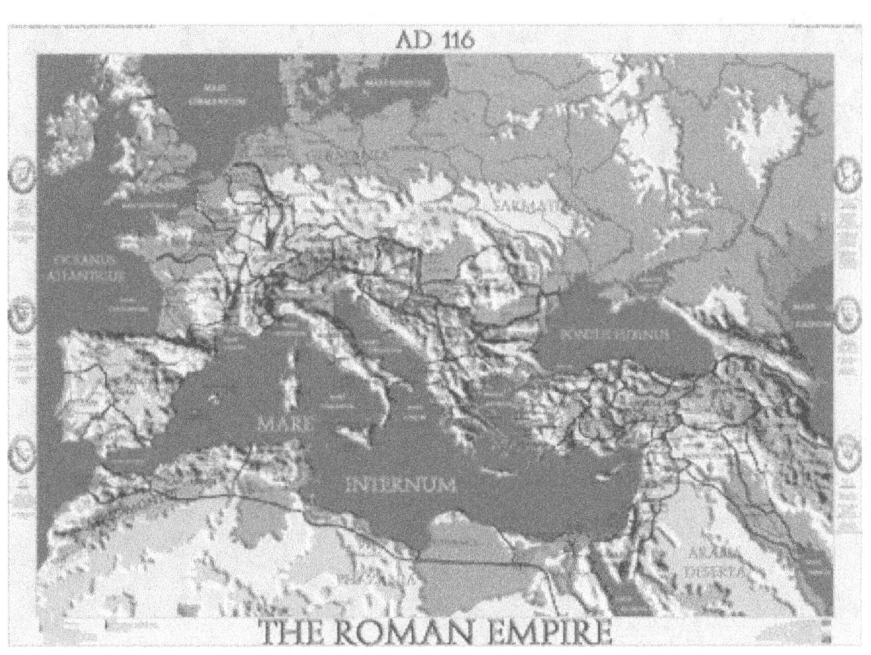

Written By:
Joseph Aquilino

Copyright 2013 © by Sensational Publications
All rights reserved. This book or any portion thereof
may not be reproduced or used in any manner whatsoever
without the express written permission of the publisher
except for the use of brief quotations in a book review.

First American Paperback Edition

Sensational Publications
P.O. Box 661
Oswego, IL 60543
www.SensationalPublications.com

Library of Congress Control Number: 2013941380

ISBN 978-0-9888003-9-7

Acknowledgements

I would like to thank the following people for their gracious, support in formulating and writing this thesis for the three months I have been working on it:
-My Classmates for being supportive of me and always being there for me.
-My beautiful girlfriend Nina for reviewing and editing the thesis.
-My family, especially, my dad, Frank who has been very supportive in letting me use the computer for all these hours.
-My friends for always being there for me and for assisting me in the editing of this thesis.
-Most importantly my professors for keeping me focused and on track with this thesis.

The Table of Contents

Chronological History of Rome from BCE to CE   p1

Introduction   p18

Roman Topography vs. the Vast American Terrain   p23

Part 1: Overview of the Roman/ Italian Geography   p25

Part 2: The Roman Empire and the Advantages of the Apennine   p30 and Alps Mountains

Part 3: Overview of the Vast American Terrain   p36

Part 4: Rome vs. America on Geography: Conclusion by Peter Bender   p43

Part 5: Rome vs. America on Geography: Conclusion by Joseph Aquilino   p49

Table 1: The History of Rome: through the use of Maps   p58

Chapter 2: Roman Imperialism vs. the Great American Democratic Ideal   p63

Part 1: An Overview of Roman Politics   p64

LIST OF ROMAN EMPERORS   p69

Part 2: Through the eyes of Literature: Roman Politics according   p75-

To the imagery in Virgil's "The Aeneid"

Part 3: Through the eyes of Literature: Marcus Aurelius' Meditations

vs. Albert Camus' Caligula   p89

Part 4: Through the eyes of Literature: Aristotle vs. Plato on the

Education of the Military and the Many Different Types Government   p95

Part 5: Through the eyes of Literature: Tyranny and Government by Machiavelli and Plato   p105

Table 2: The Faces of the Leadership in Ancient Rome   p112

Part 6: An Overview of the American Presidency   p119

Part 7: The Year 1968: The American and European "Counter Cultural Decline"   p129

Chapter 3: Society and Economics in Rome and America   p135

Part 1: Overview of Roman Social and Economic Life   p142

Part 2: Roman Architecture and Art: A Source of Economic Power and Strength   p148

Part 3: America's African American Slaves vs. Ancient Rome's Gladiators   p165

Part 4: Through the eyes of Movies: How America, Art and Literature Perceive Roman Gladiatorial Combat   p174

Table 3: Pictures of the Roman Republic   p181

Part 5: Overview of the American Socio-Economic System   p197

Part 6: Darwin's Political and Scientific Effects on Literature and Society in America and Europe during the late 1800's and early 1900's   p205

The Conclusions   p233

Conclusion 1 by Edward Gibbon   p239

Conclusion 2 by Peter Bender   p234

Conclusion 3 by Joseph Aquilino   p242

Appendix I   p252

Appendix II   p261

Appendix III   p262

Appendix IV   p263

Appendix V   p264

Chronological History of Rome from BCE to CE

2000-1000 BCE: Rome

Indo-European immigrants slowly inhabit Italy by way of the Alps. They bring the horse, the wheeled cart, and artistic knowledge of bronze work to the Italian peninsula. Two different groups, the Greeks and the Etruscans, occupy different regions of the peninsula during the eighth century.

753 BCE: Rome

Archeological research indicates that the founders of Rome itself are Italic people who occupy the area south of the Tiber River. By the sixth century BCE, Rome will have become the dominant power of most of its surrounding area.

600 BCE: Rome

The Etruscans, believed to be natives of Asia Minor, establish cities stretching from northern to central Italy. Their major contributions to the Romans are the arch and the vault, gladiatorial combat for entertainment and the study of animals to predict future events. The Greeks establish city-states along the southern coast of Italy and the island of Sicily. Their contributions to the Romans are the basis of the Roman alphabet, many religious concepts and artistic talent as well as mythology.

509 BCE: Rome:

The Roman monarchy is overthrown and replaced with a republic. For more than two centuries following the establishment of the Roman Republic, Rome is constantly at war with the other inhabitants of Italy (the Etruscans and the Greeks).

494 BCE: Rome:

The first victory of the plebeian class over the patricians results in agreement between the two classes to allow the plebeians to elect officers, tribunes, with the power to veto any unlawful acts of the magistrates.

450 BCE: Rome

The Law of the Twelve Tables is established allowing the plebeians to have knowledge of their relationship to the law. The plebeians are primarily farmers, craftsmen and tradesmen with foreign background. The patricians make up an aristocracy.

367 BCE: Rome

The first plebeian consul is elected to the assembly, and plebeians become eligible to serve as lesser magistrates, formerly a position only granted to the aristocratic class. Because an ancient custom allows promotion from magistracy to the Senate, the patrician-dominated Senate is broken.

287 BCE:

The Roman system of coinage is established.

265 BCE: Rome

Initiates the Punic Wars with Carthage, an oligarchic empire stretching from the northern coast of Africa to the Strait of Gibraltar. The primary cause of these Wars is Carthaginian expansion into the Greek cities of Sicily. Carthage is forced to surrender its control over the western region of Sicily, which marks the end of the First Punic War.

218 BCE:

The Romans renew their efforts against Carthage due to Carthaginian expansion in Spain, which lasts 16 years. At the end of the Second Punic War, Carthage is forced to surrender all Carthaginian territory to Rome with the exception of their capital city in northern Africa.

149 - 146 BCE:

The Third Punic War results in the total loss of Carthaginian territory. Its inhabitants are sold into slavery and the capital city is burned. The total accumulation of territory as a result of these wars is a Roman empire including Spain, northern Africa, Greece, Asia Minor and rule over Egypt.

146 - 30 BCE:

As a result of the Punic Wars, Roman civilization witnesses a series of cultural conflicts ranging from class conflicts and assassinations to slave retaliation in Sicily in 104 BCE and 73 BCE. The class conflicts begin with the two tribunes Tiberius Gracchus (elected in 133 BCE and Gaius Gracchus (elected in 123 BCE). The Gracchi brothers both strive for reforms of the Roman Republic, but fail due to the conservative customs of the upper class and their resistance to change. Following the attempts of the Gracchi brothers are those of two military leaders, Marius and Sulla.

140 BCE:

The introduction of Stoicism into Rome is a major influence on Roman leaders. Cicero, "the father of Roman eloquence," derives the bulk of his thought from the Stoics, though he is well read in both Plato and Aristotle. Cicero's prose is primarily a fusion of Roman political thought and Stoicism's basic beliefs that happiness is attained by way of the virtuous life and the highest good is tranquility of mind.

107 BCE:

Marius is appointed to consulship and rules the state by military means until his death in 86 BCE.

98 BCE:

Lucretius, author of On the Nature of Things, is the most renowned of the Roman Epicureans. Epicureanism is one of the most notable influences the Greek world bestows on Roman civilization. Lucretius' poetry explains the Epicurean beliefs of obtaining the "good life" through peace of mind and disbelief in the fear of the supernatural and any afterlife. He dies in 55 BCE.

82 BCE:

Following the death of Marius, the ruthless aristocrat Sulla is appointed dictator and retires after three years. Because Sulla grants full control of the Roman Empire to the aristocracy, two leaders in defense of the Roman people, Julius Caesar and Pompey, challenge his efforts. These two leaders join their efforts to seize the Roman government but soon become rivals.

70 BCE:

A close friend of Horace, the poet Virgil authors The Eclogues and The Aeneid. He is later considered a prophet of Christianity in the Middle Ages. He dies in 19 BCE.

65 BCE:

Horace authors the Odes, which glorify Roman imperialism. Horace's literature exemplifies the fusion of Epicureanism and Stoicism. He dies in 8 BCE.

52 BCE:

The Senate elects Pompey as sole consul, and Caesar is declared an enemy of the Roman Republic. Caesar, at first stationed in Gaul, marches into Rome in 49 BCE, and in 48 BCE, the two men war at Pharsalus in Greece. With the defeat of Pompey, Caesar campaigns in Egypt and Asia Minor before returning to Rome.

46 BCE:

Rome - Caesar is appointed dictator and assumes total control from the Senate. On a charge that he intends to make himself king, he is assassinated on the Ides of March (44 BCE) by a group leadership led by Brutus and Cassius. Among Caesar's contributions to Rome is the 365-day calendar with an extra day every four years, agricultural wealth for Rome and urban culture in the West due to his efforts to expand westward, and the cultural assimilation of the various regions under Roman rule.

42 BCE: Rome

Having learned of Caesar's death while stationed in Gaul, Octavian returns to Rome to collect his inheritance as sole heir to his granduncle's empire. Upon his arrival he aligns himself with two of Caesar's friends, Mark Antony and Lepidus, in an attempt to overthrow the aristocratic group responsible for Caesar's murder. Octavian and his allies defeat Brutus and Cassias near Philippi. Following the victory, a quarrel develops between Octavian and his forces in the west and Mark Antony and his new ally, Cleopatra.

31 BCE: Rome

Antony and Cleopatra are defeated by Octavian, ensuring the prosperity of Greek ideals without threat from the eastern principles of despotism. His victory begins a new Roman era, called the Principate or Early Empire. The Senate and army bestow the name of Augustus and emperor ("victorious general") upon Octavian, and he is commonly referred to as Augustus. Having gained more land for Rome than any other ruler before him, Augustus dies in 14 CE with his rule having lasted 44 years.

1 CE: Rome

Though the exact year is not known, a sixth century monk attributes this time to the birth of Jesus of Nazareth in Judea. The first four books of the New Testament (written later) are the only surviving parts. How do they compare? Other questions answered in this thesis include: What happened in 1968, the year of the counter-cultural revolution? Who is to blame for the downfall of the American society? Did architecture and art play a huge role in Roman economics? What was the Coliseum? Who were the gladiators? How did the gladiators compare to the African-American slaves? Who were the African-American slaves? How did slavery affect the society as a whole?

So the major question is: Will America fall like Rome did in 479AD? Will we ever find out the answer to this question or will it forever be in our memories? The only way to find out the answer to that question is to sit down, read and enjoy this thesis. Account of Jesus' career which consists of preaching love of God and one's neighbor, healing the sick, teaching humility by example and professing the end of the world and the establishment of heaven.

10 CE: Rome

The Apostle Paul, a Jew from the city of Tarsus in Asia Minor, follows Jesus and forms a Christian Theology. He declares CHRISTIANITY a universal religion and spreads the Gospel throughout the Mediterranean region. Paul fashions the foundations of personal salvation through Jesus Christ. He dies in 67 CE.

14 CE: Rome

With the exception of Claudius' rule (41-54 CE) and his conquest of Britain in 43 CE, the period between the death of Augustus and the rule of Nerva is a period without competent rulers. Caligula (37-41 CE) and Nero (54-68) are two brutal tyrants who contribute to the violence in Rome.

20-200 CE: Rome

For almost two centuries, philosophy, literature, architecture, art and engineering thrive in the Roman world. The most influential thought during the Principate is a form of Stoicism very different from the original Hellenistic thought. The Roman Stoics are interested in politics and ethics with a heavy emphasis on religious values, rather than physical theories. The three most important Stoics of the Roman world are Nero's advisor, Seneca (4 BCE-65 CE); a slave named Epictetus (60-120 CE); and the Emperor Marcus Aurelius (121-180 CE). The ultimate goal of Roman Stoicism is inner peace and the awareness that true happiness is found only in submission to the order of universe.

75-80 CE: Rome

The Roman emperors build the Coliseum as a place of gladiatorial combat.

96-180 CE: Rome

This period is commonly referred to as the "five good emperors." It is a return to a strong and stable government comparable to the rule of Augustus. The five emperors and the years of their rule are Nerva (96-98 CE), Trajan (98-117 CE), Hadrian (117-138 CE), Antoninus Pius (138-161 CE) and Marcus Aurelius (161-180 CE). From the rule of Augustus to the end of Aurelius' rule, Roman civilization is witness to several centuries of Roman peace (Pax Romana) stretching from Scotland to Persia.

180 CE: Rome

With the death of Stoic Emperor Marcus Aurelius, author of The Meditations, Commodus is made emperor. This period is considered the beginning of the decline of the Roman Empire. Though the first four of the "five good emperors" choose promising young men to succeed their rule, Aurelius chooses his son and is criticized for this decision. Commodus rules as a brutal tyrant and is strangled in 192 CE by a group of private conspirators. Because he had chosen no successor, different sects of the Roman army raise their own candidates and civil war breaks out.

193 CE: Rome

The first ruler resulting from the civil wars is Septimus Severus who serves as a military dictator until his death in 211 CE. His victory exemplifies the rising attitude concerning the rule of Rome; he shows that one has only to be strong in military pursuits to seize power.

204 CE: Rome

Plotinus, the father of Neoplatonism, develops a philosophy synthesized out of Platonism, Aristotelianism and Stoicism that resembles Oriental mysticism. His works, The Enneads, are arranged in six groups of nine by one of his pupils, Porphyry. Plotinus' thought later influences Augustine and Christian thinking and is especially influential to the Renaissance humanists. He teaches in Rome until his death in 270 CE.

235 CE: Rome

Between the years 235 and 284 CE, twenty-six military leaders seize power, including some of Rome's external enemies.

284-610 CE: Rome

The period from the beginning of Diocletian's rule until 610 CE is commonly referred to as the age of late antiquity, rather than primarily Roman or Medieval. This period witnesses the rise of Christianity and the decline of the Roman Empire.

284 CE: Rome

Emperor Diocletian begins the reorganization of the Roman Empire. Differing from former Roman Emperors, Diocletian rules from

Nicomedia (modern-day Turkey), rather than from Rome, and accepts the title of dominus (lord), the title of an Oriental potentate. His reforms include the separation of military and civilian administration, division of the Empire into halves, granting his trusted friend Maximian with the western half (the two Caesars then divide rule into subsections), the introduction of new agricultural legislation and a new tax system. Though his reorganization of Rome ends the chaotic military exchange of rule, his easternization of the Roman Empire redistributes the wealth to the East and refashions Roman government into an imperial bureaucracy.

303 CE: Rome

Diocletian constructs the baths in Rome, the largest yet built, and retires to Yugoslavia in 305 CE. Civil war breaks out and lasts for seven years, until Constantine gains victory.

312-324 CE: Rome

The rule of Constantine is situated in the West. In the year 324 CE, Constantine abolishes Diocletian's system of divided power and rules over a reunited empire until his death in 337 CE.

313 CE: Rome

Constantine signs the Edict of Milan, establishing a policy of toleration for Christians in the Empire.

325 CE: Rome

Constantine organizes the Council of Nicaea and serves as a presiding officer. The council of 300 bishops meets to resolve controversies over doctrine, which is causing conflicts within the Roman Empire, mainly between the Arians and the Athanasians. The crucial problem is how to interpret the relationship between God the Father and Christ, who had been man.

330 CE: Rome

Constantine erects a new capital, Constantinople, on the border of Europe and Asia, and the rule of the Roman Empire continues its center in the East. He passes his rule on to his three sons after his death. Quarrels break out between the three heirs with only short periods of a united empire, as power fluctuates between them.

330 CE: Rome

An eastern monk, St. Basil, organizes eastern monasticism and lays down its foundations, which last until today. St. Basil urges monks to spend their time in religious meditation and to submit to poverty and humility, rather than the prior acts of self-torture which emerge from the chaos of the third century. He dies in 379 CE.

354 CE: Rome

St. Augustine, bishop of Hippo Regius in North Africa, is one of the most influential of the Christian Church Fathers. He turns to Christianity after studying Neoplatonism. His theological and critical writings are extensive; among his best-known works are The Confessions and The City of God. He dies in 430 CE.

361-363 CE: Rome

Emperor Flavius Claudius Julianus (Julian), known by Christian tradition as "the Apostate," attempts to suppress the Christian Church and restore the pagan tradition. Julian's work against the Christians is destroyed shortly following his death; his only surviving works are letters and satirical writings.

378 CE: Rome

The Visigoths, a Germanic tribe, defeat a Roman army at the Battle of Adrianople. Theodosius intervenes and makes allies of the Visigoths. After the death of Theodosius in 395 CE, the Visigoths continue their search for land in the Roman Empire and are joined by a band of Germanic tribes.

379 CE: Rome

Theodosius I is the last emperor to control the united Roman Empire. After two civil wars he establishes a dynasty to last until 450 in the Eastern Empire and is considered responsible for the fall of the Western Roman Empire because of his focus on creating a dynasty.

380 CE: Rome - Christianity is declared the sole religion of the Roman Empire by Theodosius I. By 400 CE, the Christian clergy establishes a hierarchy including priests, bishops, metropolitans (archbishops situated in larger cities), and patriarchs (bishops whose rule oversees

larger and older cities such as Jerusalem, Alexandria, Rome and Constantinople).

410 CE: Rome

The Visigoths and their German allies sack Rome itself and continue their search for land and provisions through southern Gaul, Spain and Africa. Once in Africa, they overtake control of the Mediterranean.

445 CE: Rome

The Emperor Valentinian III decrees that all Western bishops are to be under the jurisdiction of the pope.

474 CE: Rome

Educated in Constantinople from the time he was seven, Theodoric the Great succeeds his father as king of the Ostrogoths, eastern relatives of the Visogoths.

476 CE: Rome

Odovacar, the leader of the united German tribes, assumes the title of king of Rome. 476 CE is commonly dated as the end of the Western Roman Empire. After 476 CE, there are no Roman Emperors occupying the West at all.

477 CE: Rome

Cassiodorus, inspired by St. Augustine, is a Benedictine monk who believes that knowledge of the classics is mandatory for understanding the Bible. He also includes copying manuscripts as "manual labor" suitable for monks. The preservation of all classical Latin texts is due to the persistence of Benedictine monks, under the guide of Cassiodorus who dies in 570 CE.

480 CE: Rome

St. Benedict founds a monastery in the West and promotes monastic obligations similar to those of St. Basil in the east. The Benedictine monks help shape Western religious civilization through their missionary work in places such as England and Germany. St. Benedict also promotes manual labor to protect the self from idleness, "the enemy of the soul." He dies in 547 CE.

493 CE: Rome

Theodoric the Great assumes control over Italy. An admirer of Roman civilization, he attempts the preservation of culture and system of government.

524 CE: Rome

- Born in 480 CE, Boethius, Roman statesman and author of treatises on music, mathematics and philosophy, is charged with treason and tortured to death under the reign of Theodoric. His most famous treatise, The Consolation of Philosophy, is written while in prison. He is the last philosopher and Latin prose writer of the West for many centuries.

527 CE: Rome

Justinian, Roman Emperor in the East, assumes the throne and is responsible for the revision and codification of Roman law. His Corpus

Juris Civilis is studied and instituted as the basis of all European law in the middle Ages, with the exception of England. Justinian builds the church of St. Sophia in Constantinople. His ecclesiastical policy includes the closing of Greek schools of philosophy, including Plato's Academy. His presence in canto 6 of Dante's Paradiso is an examination of the progress of Roman history.

533 CE: Rome

Justinian conquers the Vandal kingdom in northwest Africa to begin the restoration of the Western Roman Empire. 536 welcome the conquest by the Catholic subjects of the Ostrogoths, but the Ostrogoths resist the Roman invasion and begin a war, which lasts until 563.

565 CE: Rome

- Roman Emperor Justinian dies, having reconquered as Roman territory all of Italy, northwest Africa, coastal Spain and the Mediterranean.

568 CE: Rome

Though not strong enough to conquer the whole Italian peninsula, the Lombards, a Germanic tribe, invade Italy and assume control over a large part of the territory. Italy is fragmented into three regions of rule claimed by the Lombards, the Eastern Roman Empire and the Papal States.

Source information: www.Crystalinks.com (2003) Chronological History of Rome with links

Illustrations by:

www.Roman-Empire.net

The Arch of Janus

The Temple of Saturn

Introduction

The Ancient Roman Empire and America are both noted, in various journals and scholarly works, as the two most powerful superpowers in world history. Why, you might ask? Well, the determining factors are the three most important facets that every empire is built on. Those facets being: geography, leadership and socio-economics. With a balance and combination of all three, the Ancient Roman Empire and America are both noted as the greatest hegemonic empires of the times after Christ. The Ancient Roman Empire and America were built on the democratic ideal, which was first used by the ancient Greeks. Why are America and Rome so similar? In what ways are they similar? Were their internal structures the same? Were there geographies the same? How was the world shaped by these two superpowers? How did the socio-economic status of an empire play a role in society? How did the politics? How was the leadership? Who were the memorable leaders? Who were the weak leaders? These are just some of the questions answered in this thesis.

The first chapter of the thesis talks about the similarities and differences between America and Rome geographically. Why was geography so important? Geography is what started these huge empires. Geography played a role in the expansion and cultivation of both empires. Geography also played a huge role in the protection of the empires. What geographical features protected both empires? Was it geography that made both civilizations thrive or was it the leadership and/or socio-economic strength? Did geography play a huge role in Rome? Did geography play a huge role to America?

The second chapter of the thesis discusses the similarities and differences in leadership in both Rome and America. By looking through of the eyes of specific authors, Darwin, Virgil, Aristotle, Plato, Machiavelli, Eliot, Albert Camus and Marcus Aurelius, we will examine leadership throughout Rome and America. Changes within historical and literary evolution will also be discussed in this chapter, along with the way some writers write could change the minds of a society. Through literature we will examine different leaders and theorists and how the public portrayed them. This chapter will examine how different theories such as Darwin's "Natural Selection" and "Survival of the Fittest" changed society (especially in America), how historical and literary evolution had an impact on a society (especially the Roman Empire), how leadership, whether weak or strong, was a very important facet to the life of an empire and how leaders in both Rome and America compare with one another. Through these literary works; Virgil's *"The Aeneid,"* Eliot's *"Middlemarch,"* Marcus Aurelius' *"The Meditations,"* Albert Camus' *"Caligula,"* and other books such as *"Aurora Leigh"* and *"The Three Guineas,"* we will examine literary evolution through the thought of the different authors, especially through the theories of Darwin. We will also examine historical evolution through looking at these same literary works.

    The third and final chapter will discuss the similarities and differences in socio-economic policy in both Rome and America. We will examine how America perceives Rome through books and movies. How did America perceive gladiatorial combat? How did America perceive Roman social policy? Was the social structure of both Rome and America the same? How was it different? What were the most important features of the Roman and American society? What were the cultural values and the cultural traits of society? How did economics play a role? What were the social classes in Rome and America? Were all social classes treated with respect?

The conclusion section of this thesis features Peter Bender, a columnist and Edward Gibbon, an historian and theorist. Both writers have a different point of view in regards to the fall of Rome. Bender also discusses Rome's similarities with America and how America may be the next Roman Empire.

All around this was a very interesting topic, which I have learned a lot about, in the past three to four months of writing this thesis. I learned how two superpower empires grew to greatness and fell into peril. I learned about the good times and the bad times of both empires. I had to use my mind to theorize and think about what will happen to the United States, based on its path at the moment. I learned how Rome and America compared in values, culture and custom. I learned how Rome and America used the three facets of an empire to build a massive, elite empire. I also learned the following: how Rome and America built their armies and defenses up to protect their empires, how Rome and America compare and contrast on the issue of leadership and socio-economic policy and how Rome and America both started out as mini civilizations and grew into great, elite powers. The most important question in comparing and contrasting Rome and America is: How do Rome and America compare and contrast in their fall from grace?

Will America ever fall like Rome? Will Rome be noted as the basis of the American ideal? Who were the saviors of these?

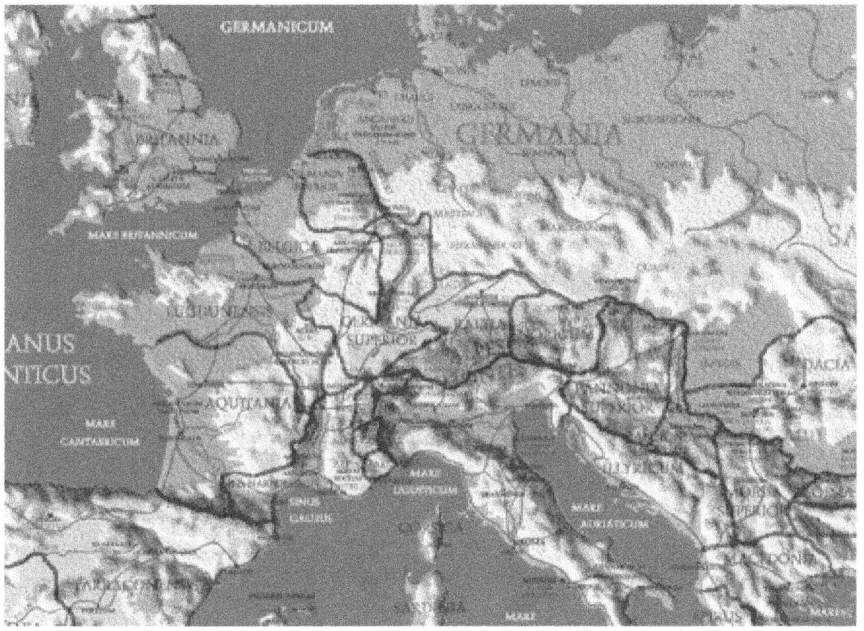

*Let Rome in Tiber melt and the wide arch of the
ranged empire fall! Here is my space.
Kingdoms are clay; our dungy earth alike
Feeds beast as man. The nobleness of life
is to do thus; when such a mutual pair
and such a twain can do't, in which I bind,
On pain of punishment, the world to weet
we stand up peerless.*

~William Shakespeare (1564-1616)
From Antony and Cleopatra (PartI,i.)

Roman Topography Vs. The Vast American Terrain
The Geography of a Glorious Empire Vs. The Land of America's Grandeur

*"On desperate seas long wont to roam,
The hyacinth hair, thy classic face,
Thy Naiad airs have brought me home
To the glory that was Greece,
And the grandeur that was Rome."*

~Edgar Allan Poe (1809- 1849)
From To Helen (L. 6-10)

The Geography of the Glorious Roman Empire

"The light that shined upon the summit now seems almost to shine at our feet."

~President Woodrow Wilson (1856-1924)
Address in Rome in the year 1919

Map of The Roman Empire

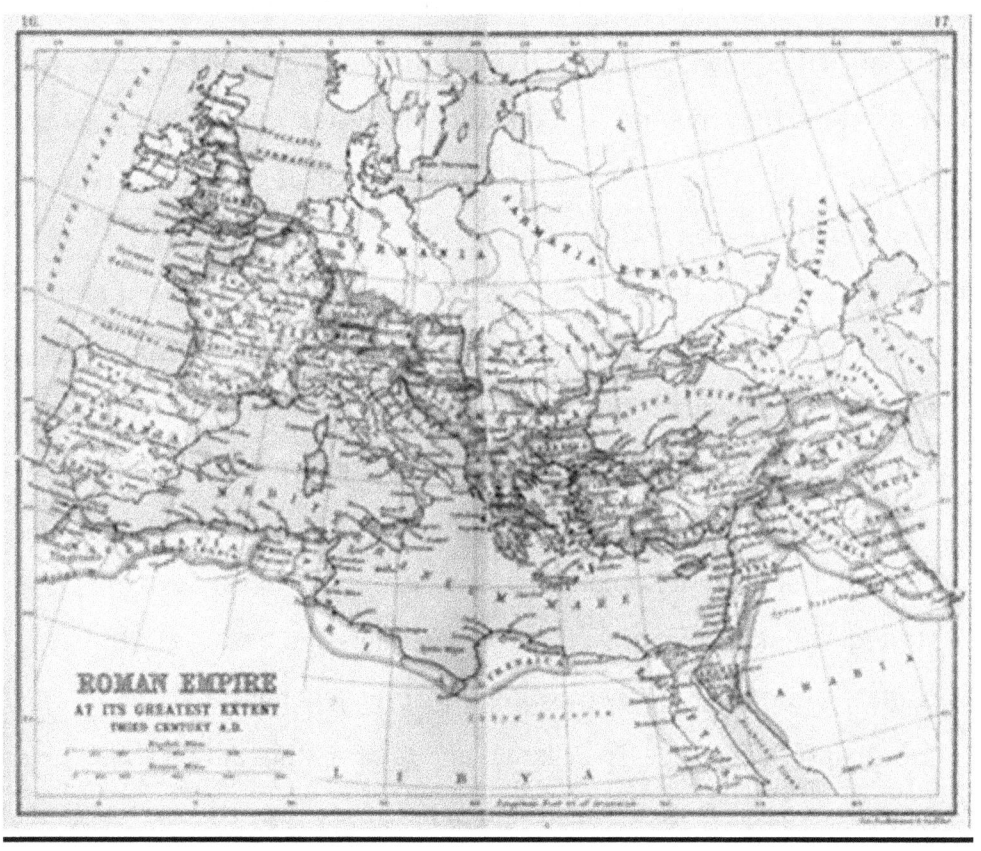

Source Information:
www.About.com

Part 1

Overview of Roman/Italian Geography

Rome is one of the most well-known empires in the world's history, because of its history, geography, politics and economics.

Ancient Rome has been noted for its music, art, architecture and literature. Also noted was the beauty and grandeur of the great empire. The ancient Roman Empire had a beautiful landscape. To better understand how the Ancient Roman people lived, you must understand the geography of Rome and why the positioning of it is so important for business, protection and politics.

Rome has a long history that spans centuries. Throughout those centuries the geography of Rome played a huge role in transportation, trade and economics. The positioning of Rome on the continent of Europe gave the Roman armies the upper hand in numerous of battles with northern Africa (Carthage) and the Middle East (The Ottoman Empire). The Ancient Roman civilization expanded because of the strategic thinking of many of the Roman rulers and because of the warfare strategy set up by the different army generals based on topographical features. The climate and temperature of Rome also played a big role in how the Roman people lived. From cold temperatures in the north, caused by the Alps, to hot temperatures in the south, due to the warm African winds, the Roman people had to cope with various climates.

Rome (Italy), along with Greece and Spain are known as the peninsulas of Europe. A peninsula is a piece of land projecting into the water from a larger land mass and is surrounded on three sides by water such as seas or oceans[1]. Italy, which is also known as *"Italia"* in Latin, is slightly less than 100,000 square miles in diameter[2]. The country can be found on a map surrounded by, the Mediterranean Sea to its south, Tyrrhenian Sea to its east and the Adriatic Sea to its west.

The Alps can be found in the northern portion of Rome, which separates Italy from the rest of Europe. Along the western corridor of the Italian terrain is another mountain range called the Apennines[3]. Mountains played an extremely huge role, especially during warfare. The Alps, in the northern part of the country, are one of largest and longest mountain ranges in the world intersecting with four other surrounding countries. The Apennines, in the western part of the country, are tall mountains with a lot of hills and valleys. These hills and valleys were good for strategic planning as well as hiding from various outsider groups that would attack Rome, including the Huns, Muslims, Goths and Barbarians. The Apennine Mountains dominate the country of Italy from the northwestern corridor where it meets the Alps, to the east. It separates the Po River from the Province Etruria[4]. South of Rome, the mountains move away from the east coast and move toward the west ending in the southwest province of Bruttium[5].

The Valley of Po could be found south of the Alps Mountains. The Po River is the longest river in Italy. The land around the Po River is rather fertile and was used for agricultural and planting purposes. There are many plains areas in the eastern portion of Italy. Plains are flatlands without hills or plateaus[6]. The eastern portion of Italy is arable for agricultural purposes, because of its rich soil. Massive farming and irrigation was done in this area due to the fertile land.

Sicily, also known as *"Sicilia"* in Latin, can be found in the southern portion of Italy, detached from the mainland by the Strait of Messina. More mountains are found in Sicily and are said to be part of the Apennine Mountain Range. Sicily was once attached to the mainland, but throughout the years it has been moving away forming an island off the southern coast of Italy. Sicily is also noted for its warm temperatures and erratic climate conditions because of its proximity to Northern Africa, which was known as Carthage[7].

Was the geography of Italy the factor in creating an empire after Christ? It possibly could have been due to its diverse topographical structure or because of the many mountains that run through it. The mountains and hills created a barrier for the Romans, which kept outsiders from taking over the land. Some Roman rulers and generals used the mountains as a warfare device during battles, especially against the Barbarians, Carthagians and the Huns. It was not only the mountains that gave defense to the Italian borders-it was also the many rivers throughout the country. Some rivers were long, some were narrow, some were found in the valleys and others were found between the mountains. Rivers tend to slow down the opposition. They could also be used as protection, especially if nature starts to affect it. Wind tends to stir up the rivers, making the water a major barrier against outside forces. Also we must look at the numerous plateaus and hills, especially the Seven Hills of Rome that acted as a defense mechanism. Man-made structures were also a problem for intruders. The Servian

Wall was built to protect the various communities and tribes within its walls, including the Etruscians, Sabines, Faliscans and the Latins. In 6th Century B.C., the center of Rome was built on seven low hills, which protected its gates. The hills were named, Aventine, Caelian, Capitoline, Esquiline, Palatine, Quirinal and Viminal[8].

    Being a peninsula, Rome allowed for good trade and better means of transportation. This trade increased and bettered the economic system of Italy throughout its early history. Without this great positioning in the Mediterranean Sea, Italy would have not been such an economic power in the ancient world. Although trade and transportation were important, the main theme of the Roman ideal was territorial expansion, through use of warfare. However, as we can see geography and positioning plays a big part in the history and expansion of Roman Empire. The mountains and the water acted as defense mechanisms against foreign invasion and allowed Rome to get the upper-hand in most of their battles. Expansion and conquering came easy to Rome because of its strong and powerful army. The Roman army was inclined with the most modern weaponry of the time. Rome would not have been that powerful without the geography and topographical features of the time. The communities of Rome were very small in the beginning, allowing for the opposition to take advantage of the tribal armies. Therefore, if the tribes of Rome did not have the seven hills and Servian Wall protecting them, would Rome be remembered as the glorious empire it once was? Well, if we look at the armies of the time we can see that Rome's army was not the only prevailing one. The Huns, Goths, Carthaginians and the Barbarians are just a few of the groups with strong armies during the time of the empire. Therefore, we can come to the conclusion that Rome's defenses and geography played a huge role in the building up of their army and lifestyle.

Geography is not the only reason for Rome's growth and expansion, but it definitely was an underlying cause. The growth could also be attributed to the leadership, the armies, the defense capabilities, the generals, the societal methodology, evolution of the environment and evolution of the individual. Geography definitely gave Rome the advantage. Water, mountains, hills, plateaus, plains, forests, weather, temperature and man-made invention allowed Rome to excel above all other civilizations.

A quote from SPQR online states it best about the geography of Rome and modern day Italy. The website states, "*Ancient Rome was a great city. Its mix of climate, fertility, geography and culture brought settlers from all over Italy who wished to live within the city walls. This explains how Ancient Rome and its surrounding cities came to be great cities, and how they came to be prosperous parts of the Empire[9].*" In looking at the meaning of this quote, we can see a few very important details. One major point was the fact that Rome was always looked at as glorious country not only because of its beauty, but also because of all internal facets. The second point was that Rome was always looked at as a place of tourism. People on the outside looking in, wanted to experience

Rome for its grandeur and ideas. Even today Italy is a tourist hot spot. Finally, we can interpret this quote by saying we can see the evolution of society and the evolution of the individual. Without a mix of climate, fertility, geography and culture would Rome be as powerful as it once was? Because of its diversity and the uniqueness, Rome prospered. Without these attributes, Rome would have been just like any other tribe, country or civilization. The website also stated, *"The Italian Peninsula has a mixture of hills, plains, and mountains that alters the climate of Italy. This distinctive geography not only changes the climate but also separates Italy into different zones. The Apennine Mountains run through most of Italy. The mountains split the center of Italy into East and West Zones. These zones contrast in many ways with each other. The Eastern Zone, the lowland areas on the east side of the Apennine Mountains bordering the Adriatic Sea, is much more desolate than the western Side*[10]." This quote details the diversity in the land and how it affects the climate in Rome. Rome has varied climates resulting from this diversity in the land. People during this time needed to adapt to the environment and the weather patterns, because Italy's climate posed erratic climatic temperatures.

Part 2

The Roman Empire and the Advantages of the Apennine and Alps Mountains

    Both the Apennines and Alps play a huge role in the topography of Rome. Most of the land in Rome was mountainous. The Alps make up most of northern Rome, while the Apennine Mountains make up most of the western and southern portions of Rome. The eastern portion is the only area in Rome with plains land. The plains land of the east allowed the Romans to plant and irrigate. The land in this area was fertile and had rich soil for agricultural purposes.

    The Apennines and the Alps are two of the tallest mountain ranges in the world. The Apennines has many valleys, which valleys allowed for the expansion of cities and the expansion of business within Rome. The Alps can be defined as *"the barrier of the north."* To better understand the advantages of the Alps and Apennines, you must understand and learn about the mountains themselves.

    According to SPQR online, the Apennines were important to have for the defense of the Roman countryside. The website explained the following, *"The Apennine Mountains proved to be a vital member of the Italian geography. This boundary not only culturally separated the East and West Lowland areas, but also provided a huge barrier to attack. If Italians were ever attacked from one side, it would be able to build enough forces on the other side of the mountains in time to counter the opposing* force. *This natural layout prevented any swift attacks from either the Adriatic or the Tyrrhenian Seas*[11]." The Apennine mountain range in the southern portion of Italy runs in a series of parallel ridges, which in some cases reach the height of 10,000 ft. (3,000m.)[12]. The Apennines have been viewed as barrier in the western portion of Italy. Being so tall, in some respects, made it nearly impossible to climb the mountains. This posed difficulty for enemies to enter and conquer the Roman Republic. The Apennines separated the Po Valley from the rest of Europe, therefore making the Apennine mountain range the most dominant feature found in Rome's topography[13]. The military had easy access to formulate a defense behind the mountains. The Apennine Mountains were used as a so-called shield. This so-called shield allowed the Roman civilization to grow into a huge empire. In my mind, without these mountains and other geographical features, Rome's outside enemies would have definitely defeated them. In the times after Christ, the governmental center of Rome was built on hills for protection against outside enemies. This proved to be important to the expansion and life span of the glorious Roman Empire. According to the Catholic Encyclopedia, "*The Apennines summits are bare and rounded, the valleys deep, and cultivation is elevated. The sides were once covered with forests, but that wealth of vegetation has been improvidently destroyed everywhere along this range, and consequently iron gray, the ashy color of calcareous rocks, and the red brown of clay and sand-beds are the predominant tints of the country.*"[14] The lands surrounding the mountains have become unfertile in the west and impossible for irrigation, whereas, the land on the east is fertile with rich soil. The lands on the west side relies more on fishing and commercial industries, whereas, most of the farming and agriculture takes place in the east. Here we can see the beginnings of a balanced economic system. Most of Rome's income was made in the governmental areas through taxation and through skilled labor. However, because of the Apennine Mountains, agriculture began to become a booming industry, making up half of Rome's income.

The Catholic Encyclopedia explains, "*The configuration of the Apennine system is simple at its two extremities, but it becomes complex towards the center, where it consists of a group of parallel chains arranged in step. Those curving towards the east, constituted the Sub-Apennine range, while those groups that extend along the Tyrrhenian and the Adriatic coasts constituted the Anti-Apennine system.*"[15] This quote tells us that the Apennines are not one of your typical mountain ranges. This mountain range actually curves from east to west creating a visual crossbow effect as seen on many maps. The tallest peak within the mountain range, according to the Catholic Encyclopedia, is called Mt. Corno, which is 9585 feet.[16]

The Alps, unlike the Apennines can be found in the northern portion of Italy. The Alps also served as a barrier of protection, in the north, against Rome's enemies. The Alps reach across five countries in Europe, whereas, the Apennine Mountains are found only within

Rome's borders. According to the Mountain Explorer website, "*The Alps are the dominant range of Europe and one of the top five mountain areas of the world in mountain scenery and climbing challenge. Although only containing 65 peaks over 4000m (13,123'), the Alps steeply rise from low bases and feature extensive glaciations on thousands of their summits.*"[17] These mountains may be small in number with only 65 peaks, but the Alps are noted to the second largest mountain range in the world. The Alps can be found five countries in the southern portion of Europe. Those countries include France, Austria, Switzerland, The Yugoslav Republics and Italy itself. The highest point of the Alps, according to the Mountain Explorer is, "*Mont Blanc, which is found in France, is 15,771 ft. (4807m.)*"[18] The Alps were a solid barrier against outsiders during the time of the Roman Empire and allowed for the growth of cities. The Alps also enabled the Romans to base most of its trade and culture in the north. This was because of a sense of protection against invaders. Today most of the industry and company growth takes place in the north. The mountains are used as a tourist attraction, featuring activities such as skiing and snowboarding. The mountains are also seen as important when it comes to the agricultural industry, which is integral to the economy of Rome. According to the Catholic Encyclopedia website, "*Below the snowline is a treeless zone of alpine pastures that have for generations been used for the summer grazing of goats and cattle. Agriculture is confined to the valleys and foothills, with fruit growing and viticulture on some sunny slopes.*"[19] Also according to the website the Alps were important for methods of energy and power. The website states, *"Hydroelectric power, used for industries in the mountains and in nearby regions, is generated from the many waterfalls and swift-flowing rivers."*[20] The power supply is created in the mountains and is distributed through power plants and wires to the residents of Italy and their surrounding countries. Without this supply, people would not have electric power in their homes and businesses. There are four main advantages of having the Alps, 1) protection from outsiders, 2) producer of hydroelectric power as a regional power supply, 3) growth of the agricultural industry and 4) tourism.

    In conclusion, we can see that the Alps and Apennines played a huge role in the life of the Romans and present day Italy. The mountains were seen as protection against enemies and allowed for the growth of the Roman economy. The mountains were viable in the distribution of energy and the growth of the agriculture trade. These mountains were important to the geography of Rome. The mountains, shaped the economy and improved economic and trade relations in both ancient times and present day. They shaped a society to be secure. The Roman people embraced their protective barriers. The radiant Roman mountains welcomed tourist eyes. The importance of the mountains will be endured for years to come.

The Vast American Terrain

Part 3

"America is hard to see.
Less partial witnesses than he
In book on book have testified
They could not see it from outside...."

~Robert Frost (1874-1963) U.S. Poet
From: "America is Hard to See"

The Thirteen Colonies of The New World

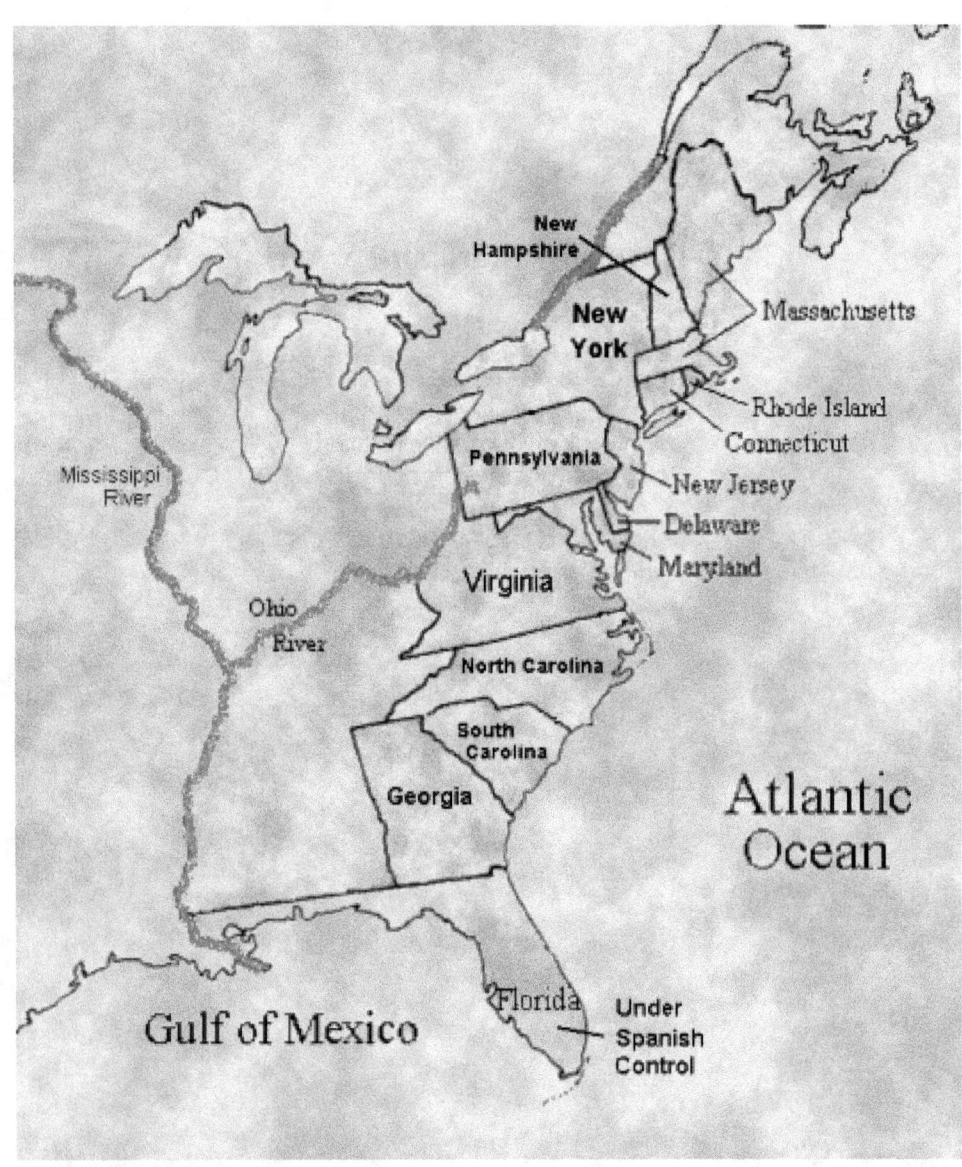

Source Information:
www.library.thinkquest.org

Part 3
An Overview of the Vast American Terrain

The Vast American Terrain can be said to be beautiful and glorious as well. Compared to the Roman Empire, the vast American Terrain was bigger and more topographical. There are many features within America that were not seen in Rome and vice versa; there were many features in Rome not seen in America. America's features include mountain ranges, deserts, valleys, hills, plateaus and plains. There are also man-made structures such as dams, bridges, tunnels and freeways.

The New World civilization (America) was small in the beginning before its independence in the 1700's. During this time, America was only 13 colonies (the states along the Eastern seaboard except Florida). America started out with vast land along the east coast, whereas, Rome had seven small civilizations or territories. In the 1700's, America was mostly flat land, with some plateaus and one huge mountain range called the Appalachian Mountains.

The Appalachian Mountains did not play the same role as the Apennines and the Alps of Italy. The Appalachians were not used as a barrier to protect from outsiders, because the mountains were found more inland (around the state of West Virginia). During this time, West Virginia and Virginia were one combined state. The mountains stretched from the Mid-Atlantic states deep into the south. The mountains went as far south as the states of Tennessee and North Carolina[21]. Being inland, these mountains played a huge role in the flow of electric power and water supply. The mountains also played a strategic role in some interior wars such as the American Civil War in the 1860's.

The Appalachians are not the only feature of the eastern United States. There is the Great Atlantic Plains Region, which extends from north to south in the eastern portion of the country. The coastal plains allowed for arable land, productive farming, agriculture in the south, the building-up of industry and big business in the north[22]. The coastal plains had disadvantages, especially when various countries in Europe started to colonize, one such country being Great Britain (England), which was considered to be the superpower of the time.

Also found on the eastern seaboard of the United States are two small mountain ranges. These mountain ranges are attached to the Appalachians Mountains. All three mountain ranges together were called the Appalachian Highlands. Along with the Appalachians, there are the Adirondacks in New York State and the New England Mountains. The New England Mountains are located in Vermont, New Hampshire and Maine[23].

As America grew and expanded, its empire became more vast and respected by outsiders. In late 1700's and early 1800's, America expanded to the west with the acquisition of key lands such as the Louisiana Purchase. The eastern part of the United States will always be the centerpiece of the country. The expansion of land led to new topography in the west. There are more plains located in the center of the country, called the Midwest Plains Region or the "Great Plains" Region[24]. They are also known as the High Plains, because the land is elevated. The Great Plains or High Plains are located in the center of the country from north to south. They intersect the center of the country from South Dakota to Texas. The Great Plains area is noted for its great farming, agriculture and its weather patterns, sometimes being called "Tornado Alley.[25]"

The western portion of the country has numerous features as well. In the west we can find the Rocky Mountains Range, one of the biggest ranges in the world, splitting the midwest states from the western states. The Rocky Mountains intersect the United States from Idaho to New Mexico. These mountains even spread into Canada (The Canadian Rockies) and Mexico. Some of the Rocky Mountains can also be found in the 49th state of Alaska[26]. Also in this region there is a set of plateaus called the "Intermontane Plateaus," which is the home of the Grand Canyon in Arizona. These plateaus have numerous valleys with rivers running through them. Also within these plateaus are gorges and river basins[27]. In addition, there are west coast mountain ranges found in America. These mountain ranges toward the west coast could be a barrier of protection, but since the country was so big and powerful, the topography was not much of a factor in protection and defense.

According to Wikipedia, the total area of the United States is 9,629,091 sq. km (land area: 9,158,960 sq. km and water area: 470,131 sq. km)[28]. Upon examining the area of the United States, you can see why it's the biggest empire in the world today. Because of the expansion, western America became more powerful in industry, agriculture, trade, economics and politics. As the country expanded, the society expanded and evolved with it. There are 48 states located on the mainland. The other two were acquired later on with the use of money and economics. Alaska is located at the northern-most point of North America, attached to neighboring Canada and Hawaii is an archipelago made up of four islands found in the Pacific Ocean, located more toward Asia. According to the New World Webster Dictionary, the word "Archipelago," means the following, "a sea with many islands or a group of many islands in a given area."[29] The expansion of the empire still continues today, but is limited due to the faltering economy.

Other notable features found within America are the many lakes, seas and rivers that run through it, which makes for great irrigation and agriculture especially in the plains areas. Some of the most important bodies of water within the United States are located in the East. There are five Great Lakes in the north, the longest river in the country, the Mississippi River, running from north to south on the eastern seaboard; and the Ohio River used in most cases for electric power and irrigation. The Colorado River is one of the most notable rivers in the west, which runs through the Rocky Mountain range, along with about 15 other rivers located in the west.[30]

In the early 1700's, the thirteen colonies were simple targets for outsiders because of the eastern plains. Countries such as Spain, France and England came into the New World looking to settle. But the Puritans, Pilgrims and Quakers had other things in mind. They wanted their own independent country. In order for them to accomplish independence, they would need to defeat England. With little resources, these people defeated the English and declared their independence. However, it was not because of the geography or topography at all. It was because of the shear will of the men that fought to make this country independent. If anything the geography was more of a downfall for the settlers, because it allowed enemies to come into the country anywhere on the eastern seaboard.

In conclusion, we can see that America differs from Ancient Rome in the idea that America's topography was not an asset. The layout of America's topography was not a method of defense at all against outsiders. On the other hand, Ancient Rome's land provided essential importance to the defense of the country during wartime.

The Conclusion
Parts 4 and 5

"This Being of mine, whatever it really is, consists of a little flesh, a little breath, and the part which governs."

~Philosopher and Roman Emperor Marcus Aurelius
"The Meditations"

Part 4
Rome vs. America on Geography
Conclusion by Writer Peter Bender

Now that we know a little about the geography of both Ancient Rome and America, we can look at some conclusions to how the geography had some impact on the growth and decline of both empires. Geography is not only about the topography of the land itself, but it is also about environmental issues, weather, and climatic conditions and make up of a society, whether, man-made or natural.

Writer Peter Bender, according to his article, called, "America: The New Roman Empire," is a retired journalist and guest lecturer on postwar history at the Universities of Berlin and Rostock in Germany[31]. He was also said to have written a book called, "The Rise and Fall: Germany from the End of War to Division and Unification," in 2002, before writing this article in 2003, on how America and Rome compare and differ[32]. His article was written in German and was translated by Yale University's Andrew J. Port.

This part, of the chapter, will discuss Peter Bender's opinion and conclusion on the issue of geography in both Rome and America. According to Peter, there are many commonalities between America and Ancient Rome on the issue of geography. First similarity that he brings up is a geopolitical one. According to Bender, Italy and the United States are not islands, but they have long coastlines on both the eastern and western side that were important for development[33]. According to the Senate Committee for Naval Questions in 1940, "From a military standpoint, the United States must be considered as an insular nation... We are separated from potential enemies on the east and the west by broad and deep oceans. On our northern and southern borders are nations which we have been friendly heretofore."[34] One of the similarities, according to Bender, is the fact that both America and Ancient Rome were surrounded by seas and isolated from outsiders. Ancient Rome was surrounded by the Mediterranean Sea. The Atlantic and Pacific Oceans surrounded the United States. In the beginning of the empires, according to Bender, both America and Rome were isolationists (the phrase coined by the English)[35]. This means that Bender believes that both Americans and Romans were private about their opinions and thoughts. Both Americans and Romans concentrated more on building themselves up internally before they examined the external surrounding countries and their problems. Both were afraid to express their feelings because of their size and strength. They both did not want conflict and both did not want to get involved with the politics of other neighboring giants. The word, "isolationist," according to the New World Webster's Dictionary is, "one who opposes the involvement of a country to international alliances, etc."[36] These countries in the beginning did not want to get involved in international politics, according to Bender.

According to Peter, islands and peninsulas are less vulnerable to foreign attack than inland areas. One must first establish rule over the "island" itself and according to Bender, both sides did that in two different ways. Rome was said to do this in 279 BCE, when the Senate declared that it would only make peace with the intruder Pyrrhus once he had left Italy. According to the Columbia Encyclopedia, Pyrrhus, who was the Molossian king of Epirus in 318-272 B.C., went into Rome and conquered southern Italy and threatened to conquer all of Italy until 279 BCE. Pyrrhus was then said to lay down a peace proposal that was rejected by Romans and he was kindly asked to leave Italy by the Romans in exchange for peace. Instead of peace, Pyrrhus decided to conquer Rome again at Asculum in Apulia in 279 B.C.[37]

Bender compares America by saying, "With the Monroe Doctrine of 1823, the American made themselves champion of the Americas against European colonialism."[38] Not only did they defend colonialism in the Americas in 1823, they defeated colonialism on their mainland in the 1700's by defeating the British in the Revolutionary War. According to the Columbia Encyclopedia, the Monroe Doctrine was, "a principle of American foreign policy enunciated in President James Monroe's message to Congress, Dec. 2, 1823. It initially called for an end to European intervention in the Americas, but it was later extended to justify U.S. imperialism in the Western Hemisphere by Theodore Roosevelt."[39] According to Bender, the Senatorial decree of 279BCE and the Monroe Doctrine of 1823 both became guiding principles in the receptive political systems in Rome and Washington.[40] Also according to Peter, as "islanders," Romans and Americans thought the same; Italy belongs only to the Romans, whereas, America belongs only to the Americans. This statement is a bit toward "nationalism," which is a strong feeling for your country's society, politics and economic systems[41]. Strong nationalism and strong sense of expression leads to a strong empire.

According to Bender, both these powers being island states, allowed both powers to develop their strategic ideas and mobilize their strengths for protection against outsiders. An example, used by Bender, allows us to see how being an island allowed the armies of both countries to strengthen. Bender states, "When Rome entered the First Punic War in 264 BC, it enjoyed the military power of all of Italy; Carthage and later the Hellenistic kings, who were mainly mercenaries, were not the equal of Rome."[42] He also goes on to state about America, "When America entered the First World War, it enjoyed the same industrial output as Germany, England and France combined."[43] Bender states, "Even before world leadership fell to the Romans and Americans, their superiority over all other countries was unequalled."[44] What

Bender is trying to say is that Rome and America, before their empires were officially born had the power to defeat any country. He also is stating that this is true because of their topography or geography. Their positioning in being called "islands" because of being surrounded by water was also a factor in their developments. Before 294 BCE, the Roman Empire, was just a small civilization and Rome had military strength, whereas, America first started to industrialize before WWI, but they were still noted as a superpower.

    Both Rome and America were insular or isolationists for centuries. Bender examines this in his conclusion on geography and how this affected both powers. He states about Rome, "Rome's campaigns outside Italy may have brought glory and riches to the nobility and spoils to the little centurions, but both great and small alike only wanted to live in Italy; in fact the systematic settlement of the Roman citizens in the provinces first began under the first dictator of Rome, The great Julius Caesar."[45] This means that Romans only felt comfortable living in their homeland, even though the Roman nobility expanded the empire from east to west and north to south. Only under the first dictator was there a method of systematic settlement of the lands acquired through war and alike. Bender goes on to say, "Italy slowly lost its core position during the imperial period and then only completely lost it around 300AD or CE under the last strong leader of the Roman Republic, Diocletian."[46] Bender spans the decades of the Roman Empire to find out why the empire declined and fell. He states in the article, that Italy started losing its strength and power during the imperialistic period, which was from the time of Claudius to the time of Nero. This is the period when the Roman Empire was trying to expand itself into northern Africa, northern and Eastern Europe and the Middle East. After the last days of expansion during the time of Marcus Aurelius, Rome was said to be at a recovery point in its history. However, after the days of Marcus Aurelius, the rulers were weak and ineffective and this caused a major decline. Bender explains in the article that it was this expansion of the empire that was one of the major reasons why Rome fell. The people of Rome wanted to stay within the boundaries of Italy and not spread out amongst the conquered areas of the Roman Empire. This resulted in lost income and a bad economy. Bender says that the geography of the vast Roman Republic played a big role in the decline of the society and of its values.

  Bender then states about America, "In Washington, isolationism no longer determines, but nevertheless continues to influence policy. Economic welfare and the belief in supremacy of the American way of life have all led to a sense of contentedness. Foreign policy continues to interest only a small elite of senators. For most Americans their "island" remains an "island."[47] Bender, in his conclusion, sites a difference between Rome and America. He states that the Romans were isolationists throughout the lifespan of their empire, but the Americans were just the opposite. After World War II, America realized they were one of the superpowers in the world along with Russia. Therefore,

America's isolation did not last very long. For a brief period after World War II, America went back to isolation to promote democracy. In the 1950's there was a movement called the "Red Scare." America did not want Communist ideal anywhere in the United States. So, America outlawed it and deported anyone out of the country that promoted it. Nationalism played a huge role in the rise of America in the 19th century. The people were content with the economy, the leadership and the society. They were happy to live in this environment and proud to call America home. Bender does not state anything about America declining in the future.

Part 5
Rome vs. America on Geography
Conclusion by Joseph Aquilino

Now that we examined the conclusion given to us by Peter Bender, I would like to develop a conclusion to why Rome and America compare and contrast on the issue of geography. To do this I need to refute some of things said by Bender in his article.

I do believe isolationism was a major part of the downfall of Rome and I do feel that isolationism did not have a major affect on America. America realized after WWII that it was a superpower and being a superpower had its perks. Being one of the biggest and strongest empires in the world, America was seen as, "a police state", which is a country that is looked upon to help other parts of the world in crisis, by intervention. After WWII, America became isolationist because of the spread of Communism in the west, especially in Russia and eastern parts of Europe. The isolationist movement in America basically said, let's concentrate on ourselves before we police other countries. Even in the 1950s, America was quite wary of the Communist ideal and they did not want it spread into America. By becoming a police state in the 1960s, 1970s and the 1980s, America allowed itself to be used by other nations, including the Middle East and Vietnam. America's intervention into these areas of the world caused a decline in the American way of life and in the American ideal. Society changed as a result of this non-isolationism policy. No one after the assassination of

John F. Kennedy really got a handle of the societal problems in the United States. The intervention into Iraq, Afghanistan and Haiti in the 21st Century are clear examples of America being the police state it has been since the 1960's. Isolationism at this point in America's history, could very well help an ailing political outlook and struggling society. However, isolationism will not fix the problem of an already ailing economy and poor societal system after the September 11, 2001 terrorist attacks.

Rome, on the other hand, never changed their policies on isolationism because Rome felt comfortable within their boundaries. Julius Caesar tried to spread the people out across the conquered territories but it just led to lost income, because the people wanted to stay within Rome. That lost income attributed to a bad economy. That bad economy led to a downfall of society and leadership in Rome. The people of Rome did not want to expand and did not want to protect the conquered territories that Rome's rulers gained after numerous deadly and bloody battles. The people of Rome had a strong sense of nationalism for their homeland and did not care about any land gained through war. Was Rome as mighty as we think it was? Yes, it was because of the rulers and Roman army. The people of Rome paid homage to their empire. However the residents of Rome did not want to move out of Italy itself. This caused economic and societal pressures within Rome, especially within the government. For America, isolationism proved to be a better thing. However, Rome could have very well killed its empire due to their acts of isolationism.

Bender states that America and Rome are islands and I do not understand how he can call America and Italy islands. Italy is a peninsula and America is definitely not an island. An island, according to the New World Webster's Dictionary is, "a land mass smaller than a continent and surrounded by water on all sides."[48] Italy and America are not surrounded on all four sides by water, therefore they are not islands. Bender also argues that America and Rome are protected from their enemies because of their geography. I do not agree American geography protected the land from being attacked and I do not agree that the American coastline is a deterrent to hold back enemies, especially the English and other settling countries in pre-independent times. The eastern coastline of America is flat plains. There are mountains but, they were too far inland to be a deterrent. Unless the navy lined the oceans on the eastern seaboard, I do not believe geography or location plays a role in protection of the land. The Atlantic and Pacific oceans are vast but not a deterrent to greedy settlers. I totally disagree with this point made by Bender. However, I do agree that Ancient Rome's geography played a huge role in the expansion of the empire. With two huge mountain ranges and the Mediterranean Sea, Rome was well protected from any outside forces. The geography also allowed Rome to build a great army, build industry and business and set up points of agriculture to better the economy. The people of

Rome felt secure, whereas, the Puritans, Pilgrims and Quakers did not because of the lack of geography.

It is felt that the geography of both Rome and America are vast and full of different topographical features. It is not only a question of protection from outsiders, but do these topographical features help in any other areas of the empires? Yes, the mountains of both Italy and America play a huge role in entertainment and tourism. Tourism in both countries created a lot of revenue, which helps with the improvement of the economies. The mountains, both in America and Italy, can also be seen as growth magnets. Industrial growth and agricultural growth can be seen in both countries during their respective times and this growth spurred new inventions, new discoveries and new ways of thought.

Geography, played a big role in Ancient Roman irrigation systems. It also played a big role in the rise of plantation owners, which in turn brought about another issue, called either "cheap labor" or "slavery." We can see this in America as well in the 1700's and early 1800's before the American Civil War, which abolished slavery in the United States.

The rivers of both countries were used to create trade routes and better methods of trade between countries. The Romans utilized the Po River Valley and the Americans utilized its many rivers, lakes, and seas to find a way to trade with neighboring countries. Expanding trade and transportation opportunities allowed for the expansion of the economies. The economies of both countries bettered because of their positioning in the world and because of the geographical features.

Trade between countries evolved with the Romans and the Americans generated new technologies and ideas to trade with other countries. Trade between countries also brought cultural and societal changes because the smaller, more inexperienced countries would try to learn and try to use it to their advantage. Most of the time they would develop a method of trade based on the ideas of the bigger empires, notably America and Rome.

America and Rome started out small and worked their way up to becoming an empire. "The Glory of Rome" and "The Vast American Terrain" are perfect examples of smaller civilizations building up into huge, powerful empires. The question is: Why do these powerful empires fall? Is it because of the geography and environment? In a way, the geography does play negative a role, because when the environment evolves quicker than humans do, it could lead to a confused or bewildered state among the individuals of a specific society. It can even confuse the rulers that run the country. Most societal problems occur with the evolution of the environment, the changing climates and the evolution of geographical features. For example, Rome first settled a land called Sicily, which is located in the southern-most portion of the Italian peninsula. At one time this peninsula was one, but because of geographical changes and earth movements, Sicily is now detached from the mainland. This led to conflict later on in the history of Italy. The continents of the earth continue to move apart in something called the "continental drift." This drift could lead to land conflict and societal confusion amongst the leaders, plantation owners and the residents of a given area. Sicily is just one example of this continental drift that is affecting societies everywhere in the world.

My conclusion is basically this, America and Rome are similar in many ways. However, they do have their differences such as geography, politics, the economy and population capacity. Rome expanded through war, whereas, America expanded west through the use of the economy and political advances. Americans had to protect the homeland, such as in the battle of "The Alamo," against the Mexicans, but they never expanded or advanced through aggressive means. Rome conquered and took over the weak countries and territories surrounding them. Therefore Rome built their huge empire based on aggressive means. America unlike Rome had a united band of states, whereas Rome had a number of provinces and territories within it and surrounding the empire. One of the major similarities is that Rome and the United States both dominated the world during their respective centuries in history.

My final point on the issue of geography is the issue of the decline and fall of Rome and the potential decline of America. Was geography a factor in the decline and fall of these two great empires? The United States, which is still an empire, has more environmental problems than geographical ones, therefore I think America will not decline because of their geography. Rome, on the other hand, strived on their geography and grew up with their geography playing a huge role in its defense and economy. I do feel that Rome's society, as the geography and environment evolved, the society became increasingly confused and uncertain, therefore leading to civil war, civil conflicts and bad economic times. I do believe the geography played a huge role, as an underlying theme, in the decline and fall of Rome.

Outside groups begin conquering Rome's weakened Armies under Theodosius II and Honorius
The Empire split into two because of the Rise of Christianity

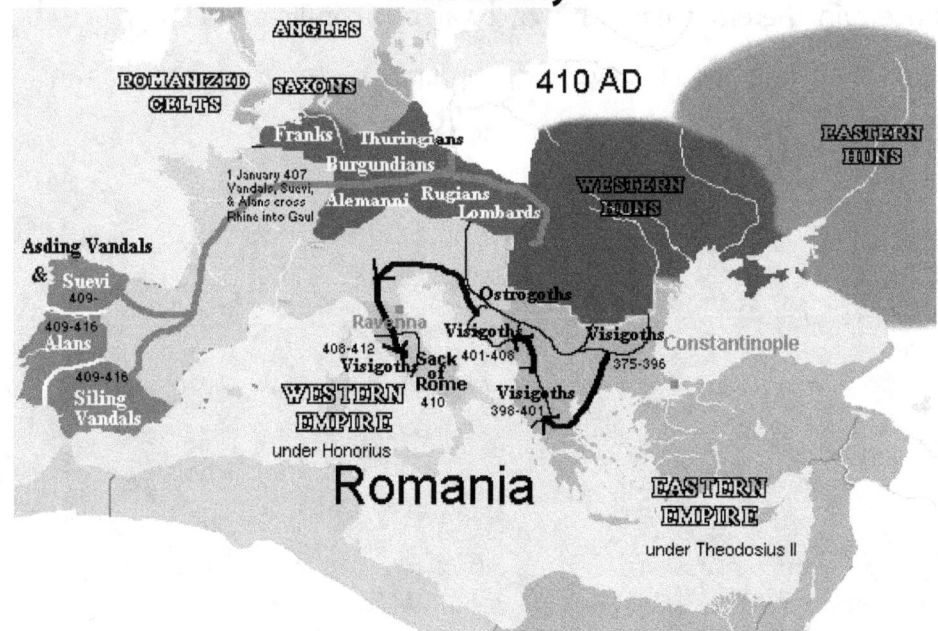

Rome is no more after being taken over by the various outsider groups

Table 1
The History of Rome: Through the Use of Maps

Crisis of the Third Century
Various groups started to take over Rome

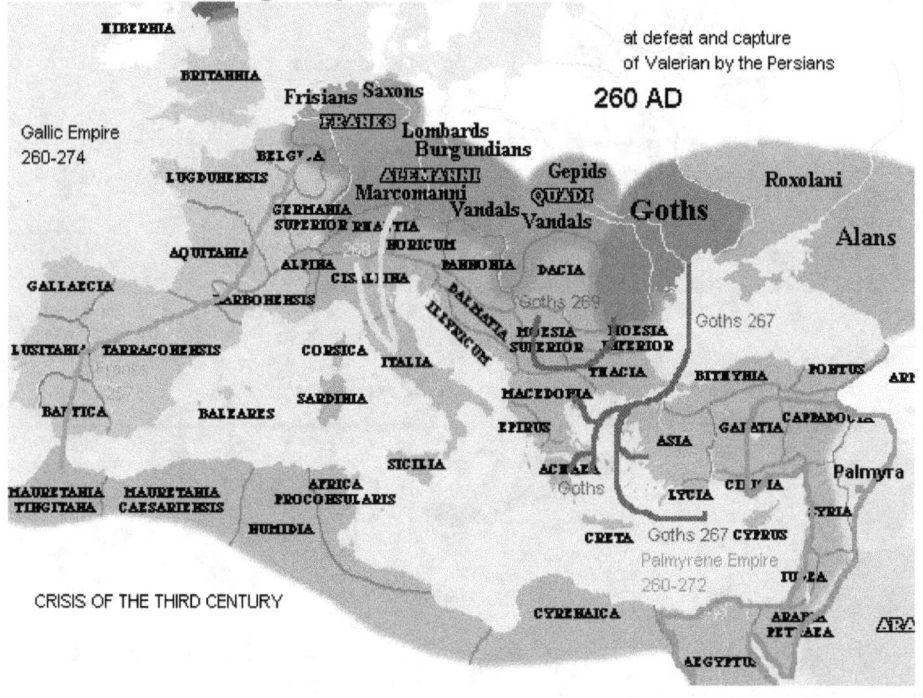

A map of Rome in 275 AD under the Emperor Aurelian who retook the empire

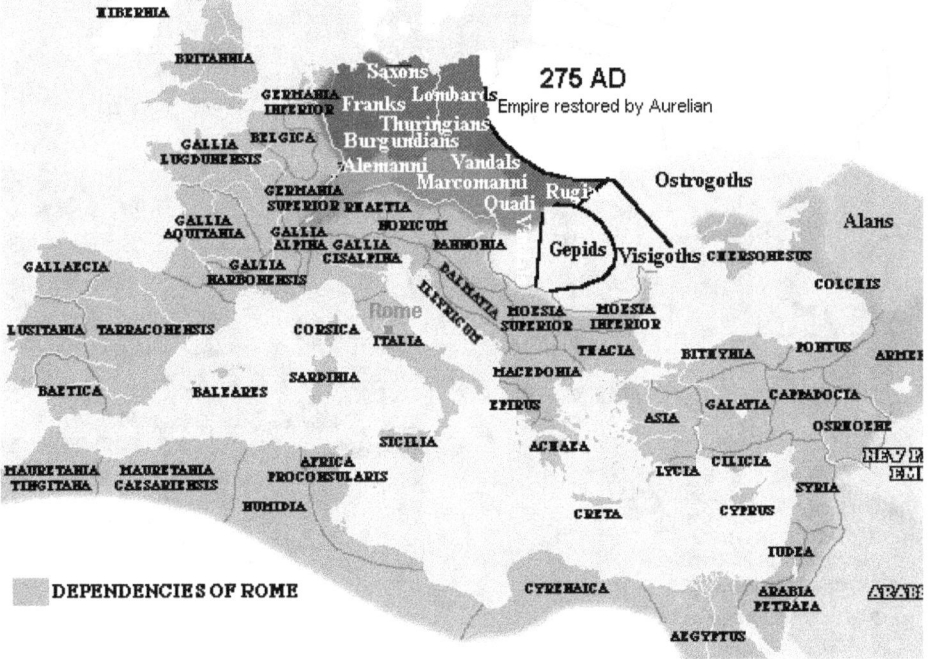

Map of the Roman Empire in 290 AD under Diocletian and Maximian

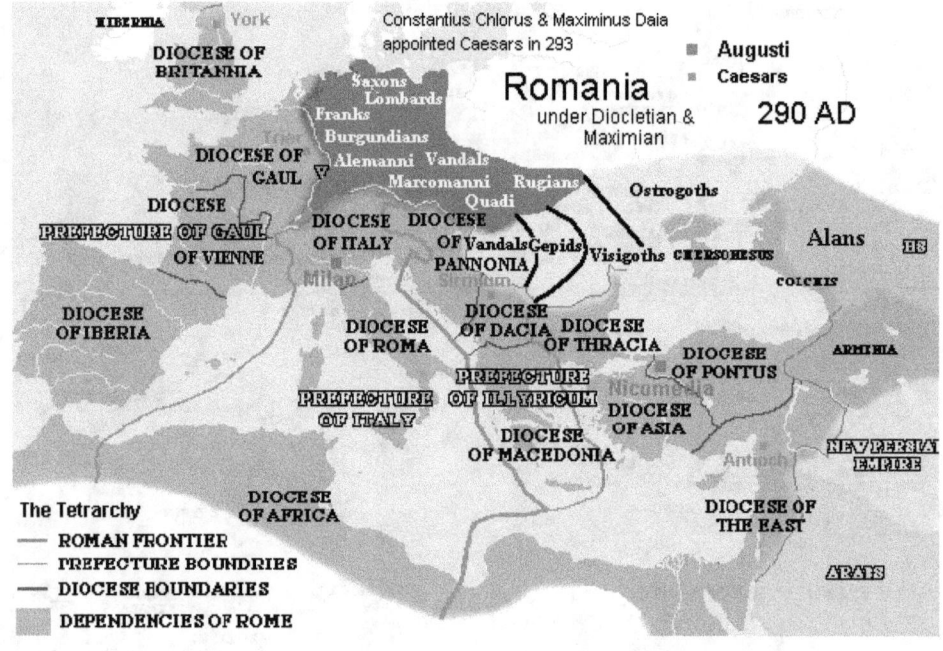

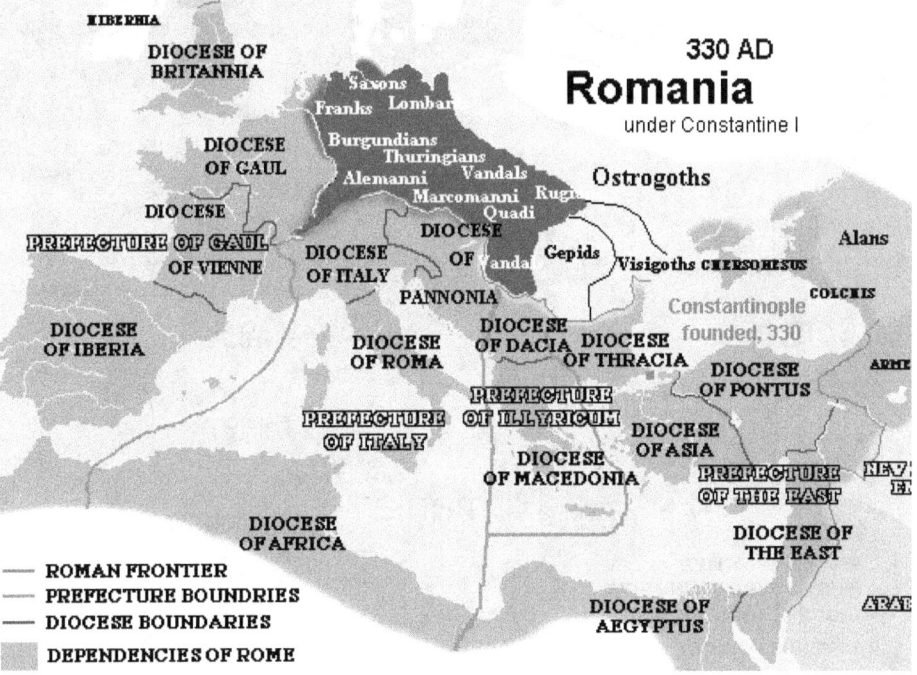

The Roman Empire under Constantine I
Holding the outsiders out of the Empire

The movement of the Huns from the Asian continent to attack Rome

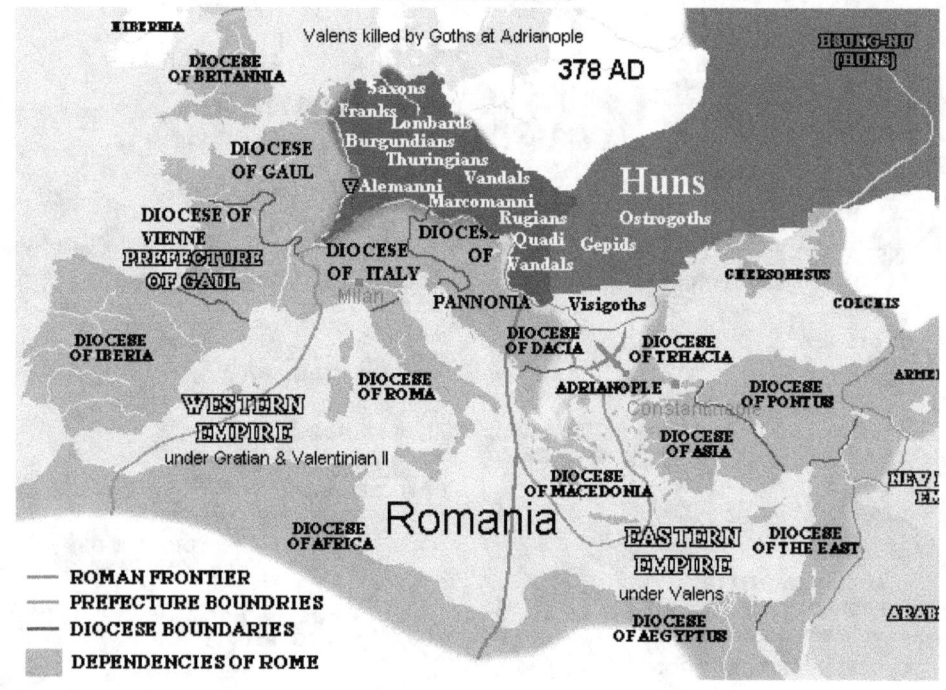

Chapter 2
Roman Imperialism vs. The Great American Democratic Ideal

Through the eyes of Literature:
Political Theory of both Rome and America

Roman, remember that you shall rule the nations by your authority, for this is to be your skill, to make peace the custom, to spare the conquered, and to wage war until the haughty are brought low.

~Virgil [Publius Vergilius Maro] (70-19 B.C.)
Anchises in Aeneid (bk. 6)

Roman Imperialism
Leadership in Ancient Rome as seen through Literature
Parts 1-5

To every man upon this earth
Death cometh soon or late;
And how can man die better
than facing fearful odds
for the ashes of his fathers
And the temples of his gods?

Lays of Ancient Rome
Horatius, xxvii

Part 1
An Overview of Roman Politics

Rome's emperors were noted throughout history as either good or evil. Many of the rulers of Rome can be seen as totalitarian and dictatorial. Although Rome was noted for their bad leadership and evil rulers some good came out of the politics of Rome. It was a problem of the ego and self-righteousness that led some of these good leaders to the evil side. Some of Rome's rulers will be forever noted in history as philosophers, who were good rulers who tried to change things for the population of the empire but were unsuccessful.

What are the characteristics of a good ruler? A well-rounded ruler should be eloquent, speak fluently and communicate with the people without letting their egos rule their minds. A good ruler should be an intellectual and express his opinion without harm against oppressors. A good ruler is a philosopher and a person who could think and theorize. A good ruler is one who thinks of new ideas to help a society and is one who has vast knowledge. Aristotle states in his book The Politics, "It is evident that the state is a creation of nature and that man is by nature a political animal."[49] Aristotle goes on to say about the formation of the state, "The final association, formed of several villages, is the state. For all practical purposes the process is now complete; self-sufficiency."[50] Aristotle also goes on to say about the state of the individual, "For the real difference between man and other animals is that humans alone have perception of good and evil and just and unjust, etc. It is the sharing of a common view in these matters that makes a household and a state."[51] Does this all mean that the state is subservient to the ruler or does this mean that the ruler leads based on the society and the society's needs and wants? In the case of Rome, the people who represent the state, were subservient to the ruler's ego and power.

Was there ever a common view between the rulers and state in Rome? In looking at history we can see that over 50% of the time the people of the empire were forced to do what the ruler said. A good example of this would be gladiatorial combat in the Coliseum. These people were told to kill one another for entertainment. The ruler of the time would either give thumbs up or thumbs down signal at the end of each bloody match. If the combatant was not dead yet, the ruler would direct the last person standing to either kill the injured or let him live. Thumbs up would be live and thumbs down would be death. If the combatant left standing disobeyed the ruler he would be killed. The gladiators could be considered slaves of the people. However, these people were bought by the state to kill themselves for entertainment. Therefore, the rulers and the state can be looked at as evildoers throughout most of the Roman Empire.

According to Albert Camus, a man who wrote a play about Caligula, one of the worst of the Roman rulers, "Politics, and the fate of mankind, are shaped by men without ideals and without greatness."[52]

Albert Camus, was a modern writer and playwright, who explored the dysfunctional mind of Caligula in a play. Therefore, this quote is relevant in matters of understanding Roman rule. Caligula was definitely a man without ideals and greatness. He was noted as one of the most evil emperors of the Roman Empire. In my opinion, a ruler must have ideals and greatness to rule an empire. Caligula, as well as, many others in the Roman era did not have these ideals.

    Another philosopher, Niccolo Machiavelli, expressed certain negative and positive feelings about Roman rule in the 1400's and 1500's. Machiavelli was more of a Renaissance critic because of all the change going on in Europe during the Holy Roman Empire. However, some of his ideas can be examined in the terms of the Ancient Roman Empire. Machiavelli's book, The Prince, was one of the most controversial books around the time of the Holy Roman Empire, showing the realities of government and politics. This was one of Machiavelli's most notable works about politics. He states in his book The Prince, "The first method for estimating the intelligence of a ruler is to look at the men he has around him."[53] One of Machiavelli's most famous quotes about leadership in his book The Prince is, "Since love and fear can hardly exist together, if we must choose between them, it is far safer to be feared than loved."[54] Machiavelli talked about how intelligent leadership should be determined by a rulers surrounding advisors or cabinet. To judge a ruler on his leadership before looking at the people surrounding him, according to Machaivelli, would not determine a corrupt leadership. The Roman Empire could have been a basis for Machiavelli, in that there were many corrupt administrations within it. Roman rulers including Claudius, Caligula and Nero were surrounded by corrupt individuals in their administrations. For most rulers to be feared, as Machaivelli said, was a way to get a stronghold on the society and gave the ruler an upper-hand when it came to governing the state. To be liked and loved by the people, allowed the people to walk all over the ruler and therefore be considered a weak ruler. To excessively be feared by people can be examined, as a totalitarian dictator, who is governed by his ego and not the society. In the Ancient Roman Empire, all three kinds of governments were seen. Some rulers including Marcus Aurelius, Julius Caesar, Constantine and Diocletian were good strong rulers because they were feared but loved by the people. Other rulers such as Nero and Caligula were excessively feared and excessively disliked by the Roman people because of their fetishes with death and civil war. Machiavelli may have looked at the corrupt popes of the church and the rulers of the Renaissance era in Italy, but these findings could definitely date back to the days of the Ancient Roman Empire.

      Roman politics can be looked at as corrupt, prestigious, tyrannical and unjust. Most of the Roman rulers were egomaniacs and ruled the country as if the society was a bunch of children and the ruler was the father. As an institution the government of Rome was respected and loyalty to the ruler was a must. The institution of government during the time of ancient Rome was built more on dictatorship than democracy. This is one of the many underlying causes why the Roman Empire declined and fell. Politics and governments cannot be corrupt for an empire to survive. The rise of tyrants led to the destruction of a once powerful society. These tyrants killed off thousands of Romans for their own enjoyment through gladiatorial combat. By doing this, the Roman rulers lessened the amount of men that could be used for defense and army purposes against the outsiders. This made the armed forces weak and vulnerable to attack. The army was made to be weaker and the defense mechanisms also became very weak. Good, strong generals were hard to come by in the later years of the Roman Empire. This, in turn, made the economy of a once great economic power decline. Spies within the government were put to death. As we can see, having a tyrannical or evil ruler in power could destroy the inner structure of a strong empire within days. Aristotle states in The Politics, "He who is to be ruled must have first been ruled."[55] This is true of most Roman rulers, but specific rulers took leadership to a more tyrannical means because of their self-righteous egos. We will examine, in this chapter of the thesis, various Roman Leaders and see why the Roman Empire may have benefited or declined due to their rule. We will also examine literature and how literature played a role in the politics of the Roman Empire. Various authors such as Virgil, Marcus Aurelius, Albert Camus, Aristotle and Plato will be examined and through these authors' minds we will examine the evolution of the Roman Empire.

LIST OF ROMAN EMPERORS

AUGUSTUS, 27 BC-AD 14

Augustus was the first Emperor of Rome. Born Octavian, he changed his name to Augustus in 27 BC when he won the civil war that followed the death of Julius Caesar, and became emperor. Augustus was very clever. He created a system of government that kept all of the power in his hands, but pretended that the Senate was still in charge. He created the Praetorian Guard to protect him, and set up a fire-fighting service in Rome. Nobody complained that he had absolute power because he brought peace after years of civil strife. When Augustus died in AD 14, Romans couldn't remember what it had been like to live in a peaceful Republic, so they allowed Augustus' step son, Tiberius, to take power.

TIBERIUS, AD 14-37

GAIUS 'CALIGULA', AD 37-41

CLAUDIUS, AD 41-54

Claudius was Tiberius' nephew. He was crippled and he had a stammer, so everyone thought he was stupid - which protected him from being murdered like the rest of his family. When the Praetorian Guard murdered the mad emperor Caligula, they made Claudius emperor. He turned out to be an emperor who ruled wisely and improved the running of the empire. It was Claudius who ordered the invasion of Britain in AD 43, probably to improve his image in the eyes of the Roman people by parading the spoils of conquest through Rome.

NERO, AD 54-68

GALBA, AD 68-69

YEAR OF THE 4 EMPERORS: GALBA, OTHO, VITELLIUS, VESPASIAN, AD 69

VESPASIAN, AD 69-79

TITUS, AD 79-81

DOMITIAN, AD 81-96

NERVA, AD 96-98

TRAJAN, AD 97-117

Trajan came from Spain and was the first non-Roman to be emperor. He was a great general, and increased the territory of the Roman Empire with his wars against Dacia and the land of Parthia, east of Asia Minor. He commemorated these victories on Trajan's Column, in Rome.

HADRIAN, AD 117-138

Hadrian was another Spaniard and was Trajan's adopted son. He spent most of his reign touring the Roman Empire, which made him realize that the empire was too spread out to run or defend properly. He therefore abandoned Trajan's conquests in Parthia and set the limits of the empire. The most lasting legacy of these limits is Hadrian's Wall.

ANTONINUS PIUS, AD 138-161

MARCUS AURELIUS & LUCIUS VERUS, AD 161-169

MARCUS AURELIUS, AD 161-180

COMMODUS, AD 177-192

PERTINAX, AD 193

DIDIUS JULIANUS, AD 193

SEPTIMIUS SEVERUS, AD 193-211

CARACALLA, AD 211-217

MACRINUS, AD 217-218

ELAGABALUS, AD 218-222

SEVERUS ALEXANDER, AD 222-235

MAXIMINUS THRAX, AD 235-238

GORDIAN I & 11, AD 238

BALBINUS & PUPIENUS, AD 238

GORDIAN III, AD 238-244

PHILIP THE ARAB, AD 244-249

DECIUS, AD 249-251

TREBONIANUS GALLUS, AD 251-253

AEMILIANUS, AD 253

VALERIAN & GALLIENUS, AD 253-259

GALLIENUS, AD 253-268

CLAUDIUS GOTHICUS, AD 268-270

AURELIAN, AD 270-275

TACITUS, AD 275-276

PROBUS, AD 276-282

CARUS, AD 282-28

CARINUS & NUMERIAN, AD 283-284

E: DIOCLETIAN, AD 284-305

Diocletian was the commander of Numerian's imperial guard, and came to power after assassinating him. He realized he couldn't rule such a big empire on his own, so he divided it into, giving the western half to his friend Maximian. He also reformed the running of the empire and increased the size of the army, but gave each general fewer troops so they'd be less likely to rebel. In AD 305, Docletian abdicated and retired from public life, forcing Maximian to abdicate with him. He was the only emperor ever to leave the throne voluntarily.

W: MAXIMIAN, AD 285-305

E: GALERIUS, AD 305-311

W: CONSTANTIUS CHLORUS, AD 305-306

SEVERUS, AD 306-307

MAXENTIUS, AD 306-312

CONSTANTINE, AD 306-337

Constantine was the son of Chonstantius Chlorus. His troops declared him emperor in Britain in AD 306. In the long civil war that followed, he defeated all his major rivals. He believed that his success was due to the god of the Christians, and in gratitude he made Christianity the official religion of the Roman Empire, and moved the capital of the empire to the Greek city of Byzantium, which he renamed

Constantinople. When he died, he divided the empire between his three sons.

E: LICINIUS, AD 311-324

W: CONSTANTINE, AD 306-337

E/W: CONSTANTINE, AD 324-337

E: CONSTANTIUS II, AD 337-361

W: CONSTANTINE II, AD 337-340

CONSTANS, AD 337-340

E/W: CONSTANTIUS II, AD 340-361

E/W: JULIAN, AD 361-363

E/W: JOVIAN, AD 363-364

E: VALENS, AD 364-378

W: VALENTINIAN, AD 364-375

GRATIAN, AD 375-383

E: THEODOSIUS, AD 379-395

W: GRATIAN, AD 375-383

VALENTINIAN II, AD 375-392

EUGENIUS, AD 392-394

E/W: THEODOSIUS, AD 394-395

E: ARCADIUS, AD 395-408

THEODOSIUS II, AD 408-450

MARCIAN, AD 450-457

W: HONORIUS, AD 395-423

CONSTANTIUS III, AD 421

JOHN, AD 423-425

VALENTINIAN III, AD 425-455

PETRONIUS MAXIMUS, AD 455

AVITUS, AD 455-456

E: LEO I, AD 457-474

W: MAJORIAN, AD 457-461

LIBIUS SEVERUS, AD 461-465

ANTHEMIUS, AD 467-472

OLYBRIUS, AD 472

GLYCERIUS, AD 473

JULIUS NEPOS, AD 473-475

E: ZENO THE ISAURIAN, AD 474-491

W: ROMULUS AUGUSTULUS, AD 475-476

Source Information:
http://www.arrotino.it/personal/romans
List of Roman Emperors

Part 2
Through the Eyes of Literature: Roman Politics according to the Imagery in Virgil's "The Aeneid"

Virgil's, The Aeneid, was written at the height of the Roman Empire. The grandeur and glory of Ancient Rome was its main focus. This story discusses the evolution of Rome from when it was a small territory to when it became a huge Empire. The Aeneid, also discusses the Roman politics of Augustus Caesar who was the ruler during the time. The most important thing to note about The Aeneid, is the imagery found within it. The imagery is what links this particular book to the Roman Empire. Throughout The Aeneid we can see different types of imagery. To better understand the book you must look at the imagery and interpret it. Imagery can come in many forms including the following: water, night, fictional animals or people (in this case "the Gods" who were idolized even though they were fictional characters in context) and different aspects of nature. In the case of this book we are going to look at the two types of imagery and discuss the impact of evolution on both types of imagery (Literary Imagery vs. Realistic Imagery). The Literary Imagery found in The Aeneid is more graphic than earlier books of the time because the society in which the book was written was more geared toward death, blood and torture. The Roman culture and leadership also evolved with the novel through Realistic Imagery. This Realistic Imagery is seen as the Roman Empire grows and becomes stronger under the leadership of the ruler

Augustus. The expansion of Rome during this period of time brings about a sense of light or glory for the Roman Empire.

To better understand the Literary Imagery in The Aeneid, we must first understand the personality of the characters and how they evolve through the story. There are two types of characters in Virgil's novel; the mortals and the gods. Throughout the Roman culture we see the gods as religious figures. In the Greek and Roman cultures, people would pray to a particular god if they needed something specific. The Gods have always been imaginary and they could be classified as Ancient Greek mythology. The gods were brought to life in this novel to show the difference between fictional life and mortal life. For example, mortals die, whereas, gods do not. Mortals are flesh and blood, whereas, the gods are angel-like. The gods were probably used as a metaphor, by Virgil to describe the glory of Roman Empire. Were the gods a metaphor for conscience or metaphor? In literary imagery the gods were depicted as one's of conscience and thought. The mortal characters would listen to these thoughts of the gods and either act upon them or dismiss them. In realistic imagery the gods were depicted as religious figures. These religious figures were dismissed after the Rise of Christianity in Rome, because of the belief in one God. The gods were also used as a metaphor, in realistic imagery, to describe the expansion of the Roman Empire under ruler Augustus Caesar. The gods, being promoters of good will and happiness, were used as a metaphor to describe the societal wants and needs of the Romans. The Romans wanted more land for protection. The Romans wanted societal norms and values to makes the people of Rome happy and content. The metaphor of the gods, in this sense, was important to the Roman people in everyday life.

Three main mortal characters of this book are Aeneas, Dido and Turnus. Aeneas is a survivor of the siege of Troy, which is a city on the coast of Asia Minor. His personality includes piety, which is a respect for the will of the Gods. He is a fearsome leader and warrior, whose destiny in life was to found Rome. The Aeneid, which is a story basically named after the character Aeneas, is the story of the journey of Aeneas from Troy to Italy.[56]

Dido is the queen of Carthage, which is located in Northern Africa. Carthage was the scene of many bloody battles between the Romans and Carthagians over expansion. Dido left the land of Tyre after her brother murdered her husband. Her will and city were strong until the point where she falls in love with Aeneas. After Aeneas abandons her, Dido commits suicide on Aeneas' sword.[57] We can see that her personality traits are ones of insecurity and confusion. We can also see the theme of Love vs. Conflict between Dido and Aeneas (Love between the two characters, while a bloody war takes place). At the beginning of her reign. We can see a strong moral character with leadership ability. Toward the end of the novel, we can see her downfall and her insecurity. This is a perfect example of evolution in literary imagery.

The third of the main mortal characters is Turnus. Turnus is the leader of the Rutulians in Italy. Turnus is the leading antagonist of

Aeneas. His personality is brash and fearless. He is also a capable soldier who values his honor over life.[58] This personality is seen throughout the novel and leads to a fight to the death, between Aeneas and Turnus. The Aeneid states, in descriptive terms, about the fight between Turnus and Aeneas:

"Aeneas stood, ferocious in his armor; his eyes were restless and he stayed his hand and as he hesitated, Turnus' words began to move him more and more – until high on the Latin's shoulder he made out the luckless belt of Pallas….. How can you who wear the spoils of my dear comrade now escape me? It is Pallas who strikes, who sacrifices you, who takes his payment from your shameless blood… Relentless he sinks his sword into the chest of Turnus…"[59]

The quote descriptively discusses the battle of Turnus and Aeneas and how Aeneas' dream was realized after he kills Turnus. Aeneas wins and his dream is realized, just as Augustus, the ruler of Rome realized his destiny in his expansion of the Roman Empire. This battle is the determining factor in the book and the literary imagery is powerful. The descriptive nature of this fight can be used in realistic imagery to describe the Roman Civil Wars or the Roman battles against Carthage. Turnus being the bigger of the two men lost, showing us that strength does not necessarily mean power and respect. Turnus is depicted as a giant in the story. This is another solid example of Literary Imagery vs. Realistic Imagery, in that, Aeneas was looked at as a character of strong will and courage, whereas, Aeneas' character can also be looked at as a metaphor describing the Roman Empire and its rise to greatness.

There are various forms of literary imagery that we can examine in The Aeneid that basically describe the theme, the plot and the setting of the novel. The image of "flames" was used by Virgil to symbolize both destruction of armies and land and the erotic desire for love and desire (Love vs. Conflict therefore seen as a symbol and theme of this novel).[60] The word "flame" is used in different ways in the novel. For instance, in Book VI, when Dido is telling her sister Anna about her love for Aeneas, Dido describes Aeneas as an "old flame of old desire."[61] Also, in Book VI, Dido describes her previous marriage as "the thought of the torch and the bridal bed".[62] In this quote we see the word torch being used as a variation of the word "flame," possibly to say that the torch burns out quicker than the flame. In the first quote Dido uses the word "flame" in the past tense describing her feeling for Aeneas, which would later be her downfall in Carthage. "The Bridal bed," found in Book VI, describes Dido's sense of new love for Aeneas. Dido at this point feels the "flames" do not keep her warm but consume her mind with pleasure and exotic thoughts.[63] The word "flames" can also be seen in times of death. Virgil describes Dido's personality before her suicide as, "enflamed and driven mad".[64] She was mad that Aeneas abandoned her and was also jealous of losing the man she loved. To show her confusion and insecurity toward the matter, she commits suicide with Aeneas' sword. In realistic imagery, we can see a downfall of government; after Dido commits suicide, she leaves the throne of Carthage vacant. Aeneas being a Roman warrior during the time of the Roman Empire could be depicted as a conqueror. Love in this case could be a metaphor for imperialism or the defeat of Carthage. What was Aeneas' dream? He wanted to be a ruler. He wanted power and respect, just like Augustus Caesar, the first leader of the Roman Republic. After defeating Turnus for the throne, Aeneas became a ruler. Was his dream to become a ruler? I believe that it was a way to expand the Roman Empire. I also believe it was a way of manipulating the people of Carthage into believing their ruler was weak and confused. Was love a way to manipulate? Love was a way to get what Aeneas wanted, the throne of Carthage. The symbolism of love was manipulative and a metaphor for war and imperialism. Aeneas uses his love for Dido as a device to get control of the throne of Carthage. The way he did it was to manipulate the mind of Dido to believe that he really loved her, than leave and not have any communication with her, leading to jealousy and confusion allowing the throne of Carthage to be forgotten. In the end of the novel, Dido would commit suicide and leave the throne empty for Aeneas or Turnus to take it over. Aeneas would then defeat the powerful Turnus and realize his dream. In my mind, it was his dream to take over the throne of Carthage and take over a once great North African power.

Another type of imagery seen in the novel is the "Golden Bough." "The golden bough" is a sense of power and leadership, held by the leader of the land. Aeneas and Turnus were fighting over who would get the "golden bough" or the power of leadership over the land. According to the priestess of Apollo, Sibyl, the "golden bough" is the symbol that Aeneas must carry in order to gain access to the underworld.[65] The "golden bough" is in a sense a special privilege, because it is unusual for mortals to visit the realm of the underworld.[66] The "golden bough" has two meanings in this novel, one is the sense of power and prestige in the land and another one is the sense of special privilege. In Book VI, the "golden bough" is explained, " A bough is hidden in a shady tree; its leaves and pliant stem are golden, set aside as sacred to Proserpina…and when the first bough is torn off, a second grows again- with leaves of gold, again of that same metal… the bough will break off freely, easily; but otherwise. No power can come of it".[67] What is the "golden bough?" I believe it is a metaphor for power and strength over a group of people. It could also be a metaphor for tyranny and self -rule. In this case, the "golden bough" signifies the elite. Was Augustus part of the elite in Roman culture? During the time of his reign he was, but the "golden bough" is something that is passed along. It just turns out that the Caesar family ran the empire for many years. Julius being the first of the Caesars to lead Rome set the precedent for years to come. One person could hold the "golden bough," as it was normally held by a governing ruler or head of government normally held the "golden bough." Can the "golden bough" be a sign of tyranny? In the case of Aeneas maybe, because of the manipulation he used to get into the throne. In the case of some Roman rulers, the metaphor of the "golden bough" got too powerful and they became tyrants. Some of examples of tyrants would be Nero, Caligula and Claudius."

The third type of imagery found in the novel is the force of weather and nature. Weather was used to interpret the feelings and emotions of the Gods at various points in the novel. Juno, at the beginning of the novel sends a storm to express her rage. "The Aeneid" describes the storm like this: "then burning and pondering- the goddess reaches Aeolia, the motherland of all storms, a womb that always teems with raving south winds…. Also described as, "Wrestling winds and loud hurricanes".[68] Venus, on the other hand, shows her affection for the Trojans by bidding the Sea God, Neptune, to protect them. We can also see in the middle of Book VI, of the novel both Venus and Juno conspire to isolate Aeneas and Dido in a cave by sending a storm to disrupt their hunting trip.[69] Can weather be a metaphor for emotions and expression in comparing literary and realistic imagery? In my opinion, weather can definitely depict an emotion in the literary form. However, in realistic imagery, people can view a storm as a time of anger or depression and see sunshine as happiness and optimism. The forces of nature and weather were shown more by the gods in the novel. The gods were looked at as a source of power and honor in the Greek and Roman world. Virgil added the gods into his novel to show the power of thought and belief. The gods are fictional, imagined and most of the time mythological. The gods were introduced as the power of religion and the power of thought over the mortals. So why did he bring the gods into the novel? Virgil, in my opinion, wanted to show the division between religion and government. More formerly known as the separation of church and state; that is seen the United States today. Was there any separation evident between the church and state in ancient times? In my opinion, yes, because the state ruled over the land the gods ruled people's minds and thoughts. With the introduction of Christianity into the Roman Empire during the time of Constantine, we see a separation of an empire. Rome was separated into two sects of people; people who believed in the ideology of the religion and the people who believed in the ideology of the state. After Constantine, Rome was a broken empire. Later in the history of Italy, we see the emergence of the Pope and Papacy. This later would lead to the creation of the holy state of Vatican City and there would then be two leaders in Rome-the Pope and the Emperor. Could Virgil foresee the emergence of the catholic religion in Rome? With the introduction of the gods into his novel, I believe he possibly foresaw the rise of Christianity and the fall of the empire as a result of it.

    We can conclude that Virgil's novel was one of descriptive symbolism. It described the Roman Empire in its triumphant times. The novel also described the times of imperialism. "The light of Rome," was taken by Virgil and expressed through symbolism and metaphors. This book explained the hope of the reign of Augustus Caesar and rise of the Roman Empire. Some metaphors found in the novel sent a grim reminder to the reader that all good things come to end. The reader might also find this book contradictory at times. Metaphors used within the novel, such as "love," "flames" and "weather," allowed us to see both sides of the Roman Empire; the good and the tyrannical.

Part 3
Through the Eyes of Literature: Marcus Aurelius' Meditations vs. Albert Camus' Caligula

Marcus Aurelius   Caligula

The Roman Empire was an empire built on great leadership, strong social programs and a booming economy. The Roman Empire acted like the United States of the time, but instead of policing and helping other nations, they conquered other nations to expand their empire. The Roman Empire had its good and evil leaders, just like the United States has had its good and bad presidents. Rome and the United States can be described as superpowers and because of that elitism, the rulers of Rome and the Presidents of the United States had to be strong and govern the land. Upon examining Caligula and Marcus

Aurelius, we will see two imperialistic minds that have been most often talked about in the history of the Roman Empire.

The Roman Empire started in 1 AD and declined in 476 AD. Caligula was one of the first rulers of the Roman Empire. He ruled the empire for 5 years 37 AD to 41 AD. Caligula was born in Antium on August 31, 12 AD. He was known to be cruel, insecure and highly-strung. He was one of Rome's most mentally challenged and tyrannical rulers. Caligula was widely known for his assassination, which led to the downfall of Rome's leadership and societal system.[70] He was very insecure about his looks and had a lack of self-esteem toward himself, which would lead to his downfall in ruling Rome. According to the Thames and Hudson book, Chronicle of Roman Emperors:

> "He was very tall and extremely pale, with an unshapely body, but very thin neck and legs. His eyes and temples were hollow, his forehead was broad and grim, and his hair thin and entirely gone on the top of his head though his body was hairy. Because of this to look upon him from a higher place as he passed by, or for any reason whatever to mention a goat, was treated as a capital offense."[71]

This description of Caligula can be described as insecurity within himself. He was sensitive about the opinions that society placed upon him. It was based on this insecurity that Caligula ruled Rome. People thought of him as a mentally unstable person because of his insecurities. In addition, people in his own family had this opinion of him. On March 18th, 37AD, Caligula was given sole power of the Roman Empire. His reign as ruler started off very well with policies including the strengthening of family ties, abolishment of treason trails, and he paid generous bequests to the people of Rome and the formation of a large bonus to the praetorian guard (Rome's army) who had helped him get into power.[72] After about 38AD, it was downhill for Caligula who fell ill and never fully recovered mentally. According to Thames and Hudson, Caligula was assassinated on January 24th, 41AD while at the last day of the Palatine Games in an auditorium in front of the imperial palace. The senators persuaded him to leave the Games because of an upset stomach and then forced him into a narrow passageway in order to stab him to death. The two senators involved were Chaerea and Sabinus.[73] "Caligula," a play by Albert Camus, describes the imperialistic mind of Caligula during his rule of five years.

From the cruel intentions of Caligula, we now move forward about 40 years to examine another ruler, who was a philosopher of his time. According to the book Meditations, (this was written by Marcus Aurelius and re-translated by Gregory Hays), the introduction states that Marcus Aurelius never thought of himself as a philosopher. He thought of himself as a diligent student and an imperfect practitioner of philosophy.[74] Aurelius was famous for quoting Plato and can often be observed in his resemblance of thoughts. Marcus Aurelius was one of the better leaders of the Roman Empire. He was one that expanded the infrastructure of the empire and listened to the people's needs. He ruled from 161 AD to 180 AD. This time was a turning point in the Roman Empire. It was a time of rebuilding the infrastructure of the empire, ruined by leaders before him. Marcus Aurelius was joint emperor for 8 years with Lucius Verus. Marcus Aurelius was born in Rome on April 26th, 121AD and his counterpart Lucius Verus was born in Rome on December 15th, 130AD. Marcus Aurelius almost always overshadowed Verus. Verus always obeyed Marcus, whenever he entered upon any undertaking, just like a lieutenant or governor obeys the emperor.[75] The book *Meditations*, was a series of jottings written by a philosopher-king (Marcus Aurelius) forced by his imperial destiny to spend most of time campaigning on the Danube. These writings are dominated by thoughts of death and thoughts of transitions of the human experience.[76] In the words of Marcus Aurelius, he describes his joint counterpart as," a brother whose natural qualities were a standing challenge to my own self-discipline at the same time as his deferential affection warmed my heart. "[77] According to the quote, Aurelius can be deemed as a passive ruler. However, Aurelius did enjoy competition but revenge was not his style. Competition was a way of motivation to Marcus Aureliu. That way, his success can be observed. Whether it is warfare conflict, internal-governmental conflict or social conflict, Marcus took the challenge and turned it into triumph. This laid-back courageous approach led to the expansion of an already great empire. He faced many invasions, especially from the Germanic peoples, who were looking to get their land back from the Romans. According to the Thames and Hudson book, Marcus Aurelius' lasting memory was the book *Meditations*, which painted a dark picture of life because his death was nearing. One of the more famous quotes in *Meditations* was this one found in book 8, "The first step: Don't be anxious. Nature controls it all. And before long you'll be no one, nowhere- like Hadrian, like Augustus …"[78] This portion of point 5, in book 8, gives us a look at a dying man worried about not being remembered for the work that he has done on earth. "Don't be anxious…" means do not be afraid of what is to come. "…Nature controls it all…" What does nature control, it controls everything including death so do not be afraid to die. "…And before long you'll be no one, nowhere- like Hadrian and Augustus... "Like the great leaders before him (Augustus being the first ruler of Rome) they will die and in time be forgotten. He himself did not want to be forgotten for the wondrous works that he accomplished on earth and little did he know he will never be forgotten because of these "Meditations." The second portion of point 5, book 8 is: "The second step: Concentrate on what you have to do. Fix your eyes on it. Remind yourself that your task is to be a good human being; remind yourself what nature demands of people. Then do it, without hesitation, and speak the truth as you see it. But with kindness, with humility, without hypocrisy. "[79] After Marcus tells us not to be afraid of nature, he tells us in this step to accomplish the job you were put on earth to do, do it and finish it with a kind and generous heart. He tells us to concentrate on the task at hand. He then asks us to remind ourselves of the cycle of nature and how nature affects us as human beings. After concentrating on the tasks at hand, he tells us to complete the task with use of trust and honesty and without hostility or hypocrisy. We can see the humility and competitive spirit of Marcus Aurelius in this specific quote.

In comparing the two rulers Caligula and Marcus Aurelius, we can see evidence of variation in the way they ruled, in the ways they thought and in the memories they left behind. Caligula was a man of cruel intentions from the beginning of his reign until the end of his reign. He wasn't a philosopher, he was a man of mental illness. Caligula had a childhood history of epilepsy, which rendered him insecure. As stated in the book, The Sick Caesars by Michael Grant, "Gaius was, in fact, sick both and physically and mentally. In his boyhood, he suffered from epilepsy, and although in his youth he was not lacking in endurance, there were times when he could hardly walk, stand, think or hold up his head, owing to sudden faintness..."[80] Jewish writers of the time, according to Grant, reported on Caligula's intense hostility toward the Jews, on grounds that they rejected the religious and social beliefs on which the Roman Empire was built. Grant goes on to say about Caligula's 37AD illness, "Philo...believes that the serious illness which Gaius suffered at the end of 37AD left his mark upon his character, and that, although he recovered from it, he was afterwards a moral wreck and a cruel tyrant..."[81] Grant portrayed Caligula as insane and schizophrenic. He goes on to say," Tacitus described his mind as disordered and upset, but Caligula was probably not mad in any accepted sense of the word; though the diagnoses by modern physiologists or physicians are useless, because there is not adequate evidence to go on…He used to get very excited…"[82] To better understand Caligula's sickness we can take a look at the play by Albert Camus. In the play we can see certain facts that prove the mental illness of Caligula and why Caligula ruled the Roman Empire the way he did. Caligula's insecurity got in the way of the business of the empire. He cared more about himself than the country, especially after his sickness worsened in 39AD. He was a sick man that killed people if they did not honor him in a certain manner. According to the Albert Camus play, found in Act II, a sick Caligula talking to Lepidus in a very strange manor:

"Splendid…Now Listen. Once upon a time there was a poor young emperor whom nobody loved. He love Lepidus, and to root out of his heart his love for Lepidus, he had his youngest son killed. Needless to say there's not a word of truth in it. Still it's a funny story, eh? But you're not laughing. Nobody's laughing. Now listen, I insist on everybody's laughing. You, Lepidus, shall lead the chorus, Stand up every one of you and laugh…"[83]

In this quote he wanted everyone to stand up and laugh at his sick and mental humor, which was not funny. He mocks everyone, as if they aren't at his level. He treats everyone else as subordinates. A passage found in Act IV states:

"Caligula: Who says I'm unhappy; Caesonia: Happiness is kind. It doesn't thrive on bloodshed; Caligula: Then there must be two kinds of happiness, and I've chosen the murderous kind, for

I am happy. There was a time when I thought I'd reached the extremity of pain. But, no, one can go father yet. Beyond the frontier of pain lies a splendid, sterile happiness…"[84]

This quote, extends to the reading audience, a sense of depression and unhappiness within the mind of Caligula. He chooses to murder people rather than be kind to them. Killing people actually made Caligula happy. So was the Roman Empire really a stable place under Caligula? In the beginning, according to Grant," The great popularity which he won in the city of Rome in the first few months of his government, following the general approval of his succession, cannot be explained unless he was then a perfectly normal and attractive young man… "[85] Caligula, a man unable to fight off mental illness during his reign led an insecure life and an insecure method of imperialistic thinking. His personal feelings toward himself were an obstacle to ruling the empire. This last quote from Grant suggests that if Caligula had the country with more focus and determination, the people would have respected him more. However, his disability limited his decision making process. Ultimately people opposed him as a ruler, eventually, the people's dislike heightened to the point of his assassination.

On the other hand Marcus Aurelius, was a famed philosopher. He was respected by the people and ruled without insecurity. His reign led to the expansion of Rome. His reign also led to a better social and economic outlook for the empire, because he did not have low self-esteem or a disability unlike Caligula. According to "The Sick Caesars," Marcus Aurelius was also a sick Caesar. Marcus Aurelius was presented with a very bad health problem. It didn't affect his mind but it was more physical. Grant states about his condition:

> "He was so frail of body that at first he could not endure the cold. But even after soldiers assembled at his command he would retire before addressing a word to them. And he took but very little food and that always at night. It was never his practice to eat during the daytime, unless it was some of the drug called theriac. This drug he took, not so much because he feared anything, as because his stomach and chest were in bad condition..."[86]

Marcus Aurelius still led the country through tough struggles, battles and expansion efforts. Although his physical condition was unstable at times, Aurelius proved his respect for the people of Rome. He also built the army up to be a powerhouse with the most modern weapons of the time. This led to his triumph in many battles including the wars against the Germanic peoples. Marcus' imperialistic power and imperialistic thinking far surpassed that of Caligula's, especially with the everyday business of the position. The competitive Marcus Aurelius was more patient in contrast to Caligula who suffered from mental illness. According to Grant, Marcus Aurelius said about his health:

> "In the case of every pain, be ready with the thought that it is not dishonorable and doesn't harm the mind that holds the helm... This saying of Epicurus should help you- pain is neither unbearable

nor ending, so long as you remember its limitations and don't add to it with your imagination… "[87]

In his work the *"Meditations,"* he expresses his philosophical nature and how he feels about nature and reality. One of the most noted quotes from this book comes in book 2 where Aurelius states, "Don't ever forget these things: The nature of the world; My nature; How I relate to the world; What proportion of it I make up; that part of nature, and no one can prevent you from speaking and acting in harmony with it, always… "[88] We can see his keen sense of reality in this quote. People cannot control nature but each person can have an opinion on nature and how it relates to others. We can also see that he is not a man of self-centeredness but a man of compassion when he says," What proportion of it I make up." He is not putting himself above anyone else or mocking anyone else because they do not have the same power he had. Marcus Aurelius, because of his fragile condition and ill health, died in 180 AD and his successor was his son Commodus. Commodus was a man of mental illness and an anxiety disorder. Marcus Aurelius was said to have died from various illnesses such as smallpox, the epidemic plague, an ulcer and one account has his son Commodus responsible for the death. According to Grant, Marcus was an opium addict directly because of the medicine he was taking. The medicine "theriac" contains the drug opium, which was used as a painkiller. At times the drug would keep making him drowsy. But, attempts to prove he was an opium addict failed and it was not a cause of death to many historians. Although Marcus was very frail in condition, he got the job done when it came to the empire and its people. Many war memorials were built in honor of the great Marcus Aurelius. The column of Marcus Aurelius stands in the Piazza Colonna in Rome. Another famous of the statue of Marcus Aurelius in the equestrian statue stands as the centerpiece of the Piazza del Campidoglio on the Capitoline Hill at Rome. This statue has its right hand extended, which once held a globe surmounted by a figure of the goddess of Victory. Aurelius was victorious in many battles to expand and protect the Roman Empire.

    In Conclusion, we can see that both men were looked at as respected leaders, but one lost his popularity due to mental problems and insecurity. The other was remembered for his mind and philosophies. Both men were ill, one mentally and one physically. Both were rulers of a great empire, one at the beginning and one toward the height of the empires greatness. The difference between the two is a matter of respect. Caligula lost peoples' respect after society observed Caligula's mental instability and sub-serviant attitude toward the Roman people. On the other hand, Aurelius had the high regard of his people. He may have been frail in appearance but his heart and mind were stronger than any other Roman ruler.

Part 4
Through the Eyes of Literature: Aristotle vs. Plato on the Education of the Military and the Many Different Types of Governments

There are many issues that are discussed in both Plato and Aristotle. One major issue brought up in Aristotle and Plato is the issue of education. To better understand the education of the state you must first understand philosophy and how it affects the human mind. For instance, can a person be multi-talented or just practice one field? Can a citizen or guardian learn more than one field of expertise? Why are citizens and guardians constricted to only one field or trade? Plato and Aristotle disagree with each other on the issue of education. Philosophy plays a big part in the development of state, region, city or neighborhood. Because Plato was a student of Socrates, he will have similar thoughts to Socrates, whereas, Aristotle being Plato's student, would have some similar thoughts to Plato. Aristotle looked at things more outwardly while Plato looked at them more inwardly. We are now going to examine The Politics, by Aristotle and The Republic, by Plato to see the differences of the two philosophers on the issues of education and on the issue of the different types of government in a society.

Both Aristotle and Plato see things from the perceptive of larger to smaller. The difference is that Aristotle focuses more on the individual citizens and Plato focuses more on the protectors of the state, who are the guardians. Plato looks at how the community affects the individual and how justice vs. injustice becomes a factor in an individual's life. Plato tried to set up a socio-economic system. He found this system to have five parts that he would follow throughout The Republic. The parts he creates are, according the book, " 1) Producers: Agricultural or Industrial; 2) Merchants; 3) Sailors and Ship owners; 4) Retail Traders and 5) Wage earners (middle class in today's terminology)"[89] . Plato's system of thinking seems almost Communist with a development of a classless society; whereas, Aristotle totally refutes Plato and develops his own way of thinking, which is geared towards the principles of democracy and the capitalist society.

In looking at education of the citizens and the guardians, we see a lot of differences. According to Plato, citizens only have one profession or trade that they are good at. They are not allowed to know more than one profession. Plato says," And our first and greatest need is clearly the provision of food to keep us alive… Our second need is shelter and our third clothing of various kinds… Well then, how will our state supply these needs? It will need a farmer, a builder, and a weaver and also, I think a shoemaker and one or two others to provide for our bodily needs"[90]. Plato discusses how he believes a society should be set up in relations to the fantasy world. Another good example of this is when Plato brings up his idea of a peaceful society. Plato says," They will serve splendid cakes and loaves on rushes or fresh leaves, and will sit down to feast with their children on couches of myrtle and bryony; and they will have wine to drink too, and pray to the gods with garlands on their heads, and enjoy each other's company"[91]. Plato's imagination can be seen in this quote explaining the fruits of a peaceful and unrealistic society. Aristotle refutes him by saying that women and people in the lower class should be educated as well, being taught the traits and values of the higher, more wealthy landowners. As in most traditional societies, the rich people get the advantage over the less fortunate and poor people. Most of the time people were split up based on class and status in society. Why women you ask? Women, because of their numbers and position in society considered a minority and thus, part of the lower class. Aristotle thinks with a more open mind and sees the realistic side of a society. Plato refutes Aristotle and says that justice is needed in a society to make it run smoothly and without a problem.

    Aristotle speaks about unity and how the unity of the people brings about a better society. Aristotle says," Plurality of numbers is natural in a state and the father it moves away from plurality towards unity, the less the state it becomes and the more a household and the household in turn an individual".[92] This quote discusses the point of unity having an affect on the household and more importantly the individual. This quote best describes Aristotle's argument of unity and refutes Plato's theory that justice and injustice runs a nation. To Aristotle, the more a guardian is educated the higher in status he becomes. Plato, on the other hand, believes guardianship is a profession and a way of life. Plato says," …we should reserve the term guardian in its fullest sense, their function being to see that friends at home shall not wish, nor foes abroad be able to harm our state…Guardians should more strictly be called auxiliaries, their function being to assist the rulers in the execution of their decisions" (this making them the leaders or the politicians of the polis or the state; this also making them the most powerful class created in Plato's mind).[93] He goes on to say about the guardians," First, they shall have no private property beyond bare essentials. Second, none of them shall possess a dwelling- house or storehouse to which all have not the right of entry. Next, their food shall be provided by the other citizens as an agreed wage for the duties they perform as guardians" (Basically we can see the life of a guardian is either to run a state or protect and have no social ties outside the guardian class).[94] From these quote we can see that the guardian class is the most dominant and powerful of the classes. We can also see that they were educated to live for the state and only the state. Aristotle sees this in a totally different light than Plato. Plato being the student of Socrates learned that the state was built on the backs of the guardian or ruler class. Aristotle on the other hand, believes the fate of a state is not only in the hands of the leaders or guardians, but it is also in the hands of the ordinary citizens, hence the theory of democracy and unity in a state (Basically refutes the ideas of his teacher Plato). Different types of government, the separation of powers and constitution writing can also be seen in these early writings. Education brings changes to society in the eyes of Aristotle. The more educated you are the better chance you have at becoming a ruler. According to Aristotle about lack of education in a society," Here are some further evil consequences, which could hardly be avoided by those who set up such a form of association: assault, homicide, both intentional and unintentional, feuds of slander. All these are unholy if they are committed against father or mother or other close relatives".[95]

Both, Plato and Aristotle, understood governments and what was important for them to run smoothly. Plato and Aristotle were unrealistic in some ways because both were not realists and they were people of imagination. Most of the information stated about the different types of government and what types of people are needed to run one were stated by both Aristotle and Plato. Aristotle went more in depth into the different types of government and Plato focused more on the leaders and people surrounding the leaders. Both Plato and Aristotle, had vivid imaginations, which allowed for them to paint a society with no problems, good rulers and strong governments. We can see a theme of Reality vs. Fantasy here. Is it fantasy or is it patterns of real life and reality? Well, both Plato and Aristotle were seen in the democratic ideals of both Rome and America. America was built more on the beliefs of the democratic ideal. Aristotle states, in his book The Politics, "Democracy and Oligarchy are commonly defined in excessively simple terms. Numbers are not in themselves decisive: e.g. democracy is the rule of the poor, the demos, be they few or many…Wealth and status, as well as numbers, are crucial for classification."[96] Aristotle goes on to say about the varieties of democracy the following, "Democracy (and oligarchy) will obviously take various forms according to the type of person dominant in it..."[97] So, we can look at these quotes and ask, does Aristotle's theory of democracy fit in with the theories of American and Roman philosophies? Well, in Rome, the nobility ruled democracy. In the American ideology, it was basically the same, putting the poor people down in the lowest classes and praising the rich, well-to-do people. Both Rome and America both have economic classes. Rome's poor were the gladiators, forced to fight and die for their country in gladiatorial combat. The minorities tended to be the gladiators, especially such groups as the Catholics, which were seen as heretics during the times of Caligula and Nero. The Catholics were forced to enter into gladiatorial combat as a method of trying to end the spread of Christianity.

The lowest class in America is the poor and homeless class, which are ignored by the rich leaders. These people live all over the streets of America and were forced to survive on other people's scraps, without shelter from the forces of nature. Can we see a comparison building here? Yes we can, both poor populations were ignored and treated with disrespect. The poor of America are still being treated unfairly in today's society. Aristotle and Plato saw poor people running a democratic empire. Was this a metaphor or was it reality? This was more imagination and fantasy. The reality of the matter is that the poor of both empires are persecuted and unrespected by many. It is nearly impossible for a poor person to rule a country or an empire. They simply do not have the resources or the money to do so, unless they are put into power or try to overthrow the government, which was seen many times in history through the use of Civil Wars.

      Both Aristotle and Plato talk about the most extreme type of government called tyranny. Tyranny was seen throughout the Roman Empire. Most of the leaders during the time of the empire were overzealous, narcissistic and had big egos. The two most notable tyrannical leaders of the time were Caligula and Nero, both who were abused at birth and throughout their childhood. Tyranny is the rule of one sole leader, who oppresses the society under him for his own personal gain. Aristotle states about Tyranny, "There is a third type of tyranny, thought to be the most extreme because it is the exact converse of absolute kinship…Sole ruler, who is not required to give an account of himself…rules over subjects all equal or superior to himself…suit his own interest and not theirs…"[98] Plato states in his book The Republic, the following about tyranny, "Then does not democracy set itself an objective, and is not excessive desire for this its downfall?" Is tyranny seen in Democracy? Most of the time, in my opinion, tyranny is found mostly in third world countries or in Communist nations. The whole premise of the Great American ideal is not to have tyranny upset it in any way. To block tyranny from occurring in America a form of "checks and balances" was set up. All three branches of government would watch one another and check one another. The "checks and balances" system ultimately led to a barrier against tyranny amongst the presidents. However, in Rome, there was no system of "checks and balances," allowing the rulers to get powerful and ultimately become tyrants

Part 5
Through the Eyes of Literature: Tyranny and Government in Machiavelli and Plato

The Renaissance was a time of change, a time when people could think for themselves, a time of societal change and a time of beautiful art and well-written literature. Being this was a time of change we can see the government of the empire changing with the times. In this time of confusion, government rulers were both philosophical and tyrannical, leading to instability in the infrastructure. To be a good leader of the time you needed to be strong and eloquent.

Machiavelli's book The Prince is a good example of seeing a tyrannical leader at work. A tyrant had three characteristics, according to Machiavelli: 1) was a ruler with a confused state of mind; 2) weak and unstable leadership abilities and 3) a lack of knowledge of what the people of society need. Tyrants have one thing on their minds and that is power and prestige over the land and its people. According to the Merriam-Webster Dictionary, the word tyrant means the following, "an absolute ruler: Despot, a ruler who governs oppressively or brutally, one who uses authority or power harshly".[99] As we can see from this definition, people of this nature can be brutal and oppressive to seek and maintain power within an empire. We can also see from this definition that one of the traits of being a tyrant is being harsh, brutal and oppressive, holding the people of a given society captive in their own empire.

In order to answer our question about tyranny in society, we must look at two books ("The Prince" by Machiavelli and "The Republic" by Plato). Machiavelli wrote The Prince as a practical guide to ruling a nation or empire. It is about different kinds of governments and how these governments survive in society. The scope of the book is to understand autocratic regimes, not democratic / republican regimes. The chapters of the Prince show us a detailed description of the hierarchy of government through the use of examining different princes and principalities. Chapter 3 of the Prince describes how to maintain the principalities, especially those annexed or newly created from another power. Chapters IV through XIV are looked at as the heart of the novel, because this part of the book explores the advantages and disadvantages of a particular leader or ruler, especially those who support the ways of tyranny. These chapters have many different themes including the following prevalent ones; how to acquire and hold various states, how to deal with civil strife and internal problems, how to make alliances with other surrounding empires or nations around you and mostly importantly how to maintain a strong military. Chapters XV through XXIII are the chapters where Machiavelli describes the prince, ruler and/or leader himself. The internal personality traits of a prince are seen throughout these chapters and it also explains what a ruler needs to have to succeed in his reign. Tyrannical rulers are the focus of this portion of the book. The final chapters of this book XXIV and XXVI are more historical in comparison to the earlier chapters, which talk more about personality and government. The historical views look more at the disunity of Italy and the failure of the rulers of Rome to bring Italy back together and out of this confused state.

According to the Merriam-Webster's Dictionary the word tyranny means the following, "oppressive power; the rule of authority of a tyrant; government in which absolute power is vested in a single ruler; a tyrannical act of government".[100] The power of oppression is described in both *The Prince* and *The Republic*. Plato states about Tyranny in Part IX, Book VIII in *The Republic*:

" A democratic society in its thirst for liberty may fall under the influence of bad leaders, who intoxicate it with excessive quantities of neat spirit; and then, unless the authorities are very mild and give it a lot of liberty, it will curse them to oligarchs and punish them".[101]

This means that if people keep pushing for liberty in their society they may elect or appoint a leader who will oppress them of that liberty and the government will fall into the hands of the oligarchy or into the hands of tyrant. It will not be democratic and free willed anymore; furthermore the people of the society will be in a confused state of mind while being oppressed by a power hungry leader. According to the Merriam-Webster's Dictionary the definition of the word oligarchy is "a government in which power is in the hands of the few; the group holding power in such a state".[102] In some ways, oligarchy is worse than tyranny. In this case a group of tyrants are running the nation and this could cause more oppression and more confusion within the state.

Plato describes Liberty as, "the greatest merit of democratic society, and for that reason it's only society fit for a man of free spirit to live in".[103] Liberty is what a democratic country is based on. Life, Liberty and the Pursuit of Happiness are the ideals of every democratic society. Oligarchy and tyranny lack these principles.

One of the themes of Machiavelli's book, *The Prince*, is the theme of Goodwill vs. Hatred. One of the most important ideals of this Machiavellian book is the point that, "…his people should not hate a prince and it is not necessary for him to be loved but it is better for him to be feared." Being hated could cause a prince's downfall from power. To be feared is better than being hated. To be loved is good but you do not want people in the society to walk all over you and take advantage of you. Some examples of leaders in history that fit the personality of an elite, philosophical leader include: Augustus, Marcus Aurelius, Constantine (The First Roman Empire) and Charlemagne (The Holy Roman Empire). The peoples' goodwill is always the best defense against domestic insurrection and foreign aggression. Goodwill, unlike hatred, is a political instrument that would ensure stability of a prince's reign in a country or empire. Plato, in his book, agrees with Machiavelli in saying that a leader should have knowledge and a thought of free will and philosophy in his rule. Education was a major theme of The Republic, which was seen throughout Part IV. Plato states the following through a metaphor about tyranny in Book IV:

"It would be the most dreadful disgrace for Shepard to keep sheep-dogs so badly bred and trained, that disobedience or hunger or some bad trait or other led them to worry the sheep and behave more like wolves than dogs'…..We must therefore take every possible precaution to prevent our auxiliaries treating our citizens like that because of their superior strength". [104]

Plato agrees that a ruler should be feared in order to run a country right. He also agrees that a ruler should not get too powerful to the point of tyranny and oppression over others. Therefore, Plato feels education of the people and its rulers is very important to keep a country moving forward. The Roman Empire was filled of tyrants according to Machiavelli in his discourses portion of The Prince. He states about these tyrants, through use of examples, "He will also see that the Western and Eastern armies were not enough to save Caligula, Nero, Vitellius and many other wretched emperors from the enemies which their evil habits and their wicked lives had aroused" .[105] He states that there were good emperors as well, "He will observe that Titus, Nerva, Trajan, Hadrian, Antoninus and Marcus Aurelius did not need Praetorian guards or masses of troops to protect them, because their own good behavior, the good will of the people and the love of the Senate protected them".[106] He goes on to say the following about the period between Nerva and Marcus Aurelius, "Therefore, let a prince consider the period between Nerva and Marcus Aurelius and compare it with the one preceding it and the one following it…Then let him choose in which of these he would have preferred to live in or in which he would have preferred to rule".[107] As we can see from these examples, the ruling can be both tyrannical and philosophical. Marcus Aurelius was an example of good ruler with a philosophical background and good military strategies. Caligula was an example of tyrant, or a bad ruler, because he was more oppressive to the people of Rome and did not respect the Senate and the voice of the people. In the case of Plato, as well as, Machiavelli, to educate was one of the most important qualities of the ruling class. If the ruling class were not educated, it would end up being oppressive and also be selfish and power hungry. Machiavelli describes the good ruling class and the oppressive tyrannical class with the following comments:

"In the period ruled by the good emperors, he will see the ruler secure among secure citizens; he will see a Senate enjoying its authority; magistrates enjoying their honors; wealthy citizens enjoying their wealth; tranquility and well-being everywhere; he will see a golden age in which every man hold and defend any opinion he likes; finally, he will see the world in triumph"

".... examine the times of the other emperors (evil), he will see them wracked by savage wars, torn by seditions, by cruelty in peace and war alike; he will see many princes perish by the sword; many civil and foreign wars".[108]

From these comments made by Machiavelli, we can see the differences between a democratic society and oppressive society. We can also see that war is more prevalent under tyrant rule rather than philosophical rule. Peace and tranquility prevail in under philosophical rule. However, on the other hand, protest and civil war dominates under tyrant rule.

    Critical essays have been written about both Plato and Machiavelli in the past years, either disputing or agreeing with the two authors of the middle ages. One such critic is Dr. Mary Walsh of The University of Canberra located on the continent of Australia. She wrote a paper entitled" Machiavelli, Politics and the Public Realm." This paper brings political realism to light, in Machiavelli's book The Prince and it also gives us a little background on the history and politics of the time. This paper, also discusses how the public realm was affected by Machiavelli and by specific rulers of the time, especially rulers who were tyrants. Ms. Walsh states, "*The Prince* is widely considered to be the greatest book ever written on politics." She also states that "It differs from classic political texts such as Plato's *Republic* or Augustine's *The City of God.*[109] In my opinion, I would say Machiavelli and Plato are only different in their writing styles. Plato was more imaginative and more creative in his thinking, whereas, Machiavelli wrote more realistically and from experience. Plato was more theoretical and fantasy minded compared to Machiavelli's writing on real life events. According to Machiavelli, on page 61 of his work, he states, 'I may be held presumptuous, especially since in disputing this matter I depart from the orders of others… it has appeared to me more fitting to go directly to the effectual truth to the thing than to the imagination of It."[110] Ms. Walsh believes that above all things, *"Machiavelli argues that politics has its own rules that are not limited by other spheres and that politics should not be limited by anything that is not political"*.[111] Basically this means that politics is in a place by itself. Economics, social problems, geography, environment and other main facets of life in an empire should not have a bearing on it. The politics of an empire is elite to according to Walsh. Machiavelli, being in a historical time of civil war and oppression wanted to see change and this is the way he looked at politics. In a way you can say that this book is like a bible to political life. Everything talked about in the book stems from the realism of a political ideology and thought. Walsh states, "Many commentators on Machiavelli understand his hard edge realism as an empirical and scientific treatment of politics, especially the politics of power".[112] The book is comprised of twenty-six chapters and each chapter covers a different aspect of government. According to Walsh, the first eleven chapters discuss kinds of principalities, chapters twelve through fourteen discuss conquest and arts of war (being strategic and experienced in arts of warfare), chapters fifteen through twenty-three discuss new morality based on conquest and the final three chapters depict a man both as object and subject of knowledge (this is where I see a similarity in both Plato and Machiavelli).[113] This education is where we can determine who will be the philosophical leaders and who will be the tyrants. The lack of education means that the leader will have a lack of knowledge about the society and do things in society that will benefit him and not the rest of his people.

Walsh states in her conclusion that, "Machiavelli was unique because he rediscovered the centrality of the foundation in his own rediscovery of Rome and the importance it attributed to freedom." She also states, "Machiavelli went to great lengths to restore the dignity of the political, the public realm and freedom…He stood at the crossroads of the early modern and modern period and was the greatest early modern political theorist in the tradition of western political thought".[114] Plato and Machiavelli are different in many ways, but they do have that one similarity which is what they believe to be most important in a leadership and that is education and knowledge. Plato and Machiavelli were great theorists of their times, one of the early modern traditions and one from ancient Greek societies. Plato and Machiavelli had the same idea of a political structure but one talked was about it through imagination and the other talking about it through realism. Both writers are still criticized today for their theories.

Table 2
The Faces of the Leadership in Ancient Rome

First Leader of the Roman World Augustus Caesar

The Emperor Tiberius (2nd leader of Rome)

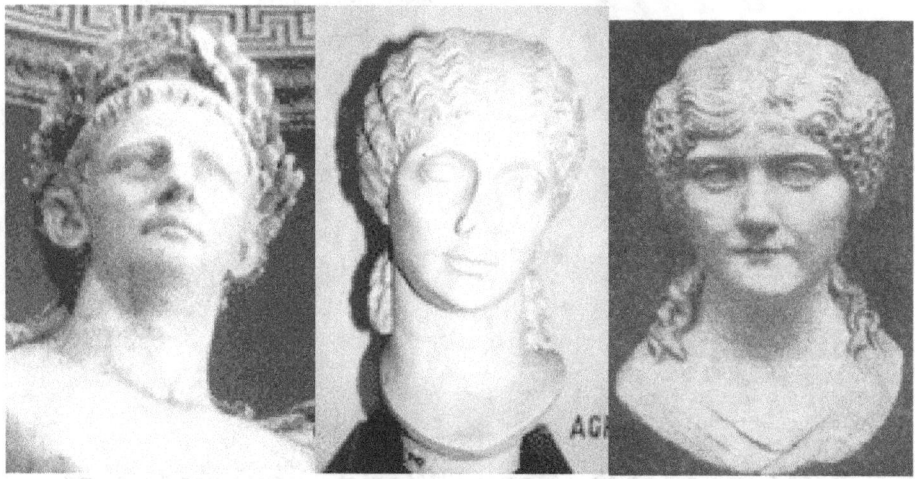

The Emperor Claudius with Agrippina the Elder and Agrippina the Younger

The evil emperor Nero son of Agrippina

The Emperor Vespasian

The Emperor Titus

Another evil emperor Domitian

The Emperor Nerva (started the turning point in Rome)

The Emperor Trajan (another good ruler)

The Emperor Hadrian

The Emperor Commodus, the son of Marcus

One of the saviors of Rome, Diocletian

The American Presidency
Parts 6 and 7

The biggest difference between ancient Rome and the USA is that in Rome the common man was treated like a dog. In America he sets the tone. This is the first country where the common man could stand erect.

I.F. (Isidor Feinstein) Stone (1907–1989), U.S. author
Quoted in Clive James, "Postcard from Washington," Flying Visits (1984).

Part 6
An Overview of the American Presidency

The American Presidency was one of ups and downs. In the late 1700's, after the Revolutionary War, the American Presidency was one of wonder and prestige. American Presidents were looked at differently by the world and these presidents would be the first group of leaders to run a country without using tyrannical means. The Presidents were not tyrants they were true leaders who were corrupt. The corruption could be seen since the beginning. From the First President George Washington to the present President George W. Bush, corruption is embedded in government.

The governments of both Rome and America are both similar and different in many ways. The structure of both governments was totally different. Although Rome had a judicial system and legislature, these parts of the government did not have any say in the governing of the empire. If a major issue was brought before the judicial system or the legislature the ruler would make it known. There was no "checks and balance" system between the branches of government like the United States has implemented. The other branches, in the United States government, check the president. By balancing the power of the country, between all three branches of government, no one branch was too powerful. The Senators in Rome did not have much say because most of the rulers of Rome were tyrannical and did not allow the Senate to run the country.

The presidents of the United States are elected into office in a process called the "Electoral College." This "Electoral College" is based upon the amount of representatives in the House of Representatives. Whoever gets the most votes in each state is the "winner takes all" of that state. The popular vote is not counted as heavily as the "electoral college" vote. Some presidents, especially most recently, George W. Bush won the election based on the "Electoral College" vote, but lost the popular vote to Democrat Al Gore. It is possible to win the "Electoral College" and lose the popular vote. Rome did not have an Electoral College, Rome did not even have a popular vote of the people. The Senate and most of the time these rulers had heirs to the throne, such as the Caesars, appointed the rulers of Rome. The Senate would appoint these rulers, in the case; there was no heir to the throne. This led to mass confusion and more tyrannical leaders. For instance, the leaders after Tiberius Caesar were all Caesars but they were tyrannical in nature, leading to the confusion in the government and the downfall of the government's infrastructure.

Another difference between these two superpowers was themes of government. Although, Rome and America both had the theme of expansion and strengthening of the armed forces for defense purposes, Rome had something that America would never have. That is the legacy of being the first world superpower based on political, economic and social means. America comes in a close second to Rome, but will never have a better legacy and history like the "Light of the World" had in the first, three centuries. "The Light of the World," would be the height of the Roman Empire's greatness. Rome's legacy lives on today through ancient artifacts found all over Europe and the Middle East. Rome had the first powerful army and legion. Rome had the first structure of government and the United States modeled that structure. Rome had the philosophers such as Marcus Aurelius. The legacy and history will never be forgotten by anyone in today's world. Rome's history gave America its basis of knowledge about creating a superpower. America used Rome's ideas to build an infrastructure, around something that Rome didn't have, which is the Democratic ideal.

    Upon examining the infrastructure of Rome, we can explore the similarity to the United States. Washington D.C. like Rome shares the importance of having all buildings in one capital city. The buildings are in a formation of importance such as the building setup in the Ancient Roman Forum Romanum. There are also monuments commemorating important leaders of the empire such as in Rome. It was a way to pay homage to the great leaders of the empire. Memorials for the armed forces service men and women are also seen in America, something that was not thought of in Roman times.

    In looking at the leadership of both superpowers, we see numerous occasions of triumph and many of times of failure. Some times of triumph in America, stated by Michael Beschloss' include the following: the United States landing on the moon in 1969, The Roaring 20's, The Fabulous 50's, the struggle for women's and civil rights from the 1920's through today, Lyndon Baines Johnson's Great Society Program, the signing of the Declaration of Independence, The formation of the Constitution and Bill of Rights and the election of some important leaders in this country's history (George Washington, Abraham Lincoln, Franklin Delano Roosevelt). Along with the good unfortunately comes the bad and here are some of the worst things to happen in this country since the beginning, according to Michael Beschloss: the American Civil War and the break up of the union, the assassination of presidents and important leaders (Abraham Lincoln, John F. Kennedy, William McKinley), the beginning of the counter culture revolution in the 1960's, the slave trade, World War I and World War II, the Vietnam War, the Iraq War, the Great Depression of the 1930's and the Stock Market Crash of 1929.[115] Rome also had its share of ups and downs: the expansion of the empire, the strengthening of the army, the philosophers, the artists, the discoveries, the inventions, the assassination of various rulers (Julius Caesar, Claudius, Marcus Aurelius, Caligula), the Gladiators and the slave trade, the corruption of government, tyranny in government and self-righteous rulers.

  The American presidency has been tarnished by corruption on numerous occasions. Corruption makes its way into all governmental agencies. This corruption, on numerous occasions has been seen leaking into the society. This is what leads the people to mistrust their government. Mistrusting one's government leads to protest and even civil war. This was seen numerous times in history, especially during the Civil War Era and the Era of the Counter Culture Revolution. Sometimes the corruption could lead to the assassination attempt on a president. Numerous presidents have been killed in office, none more famous than the last one killed, John F Kennedy.

Like Rome's rulers, there were strong and weak presidents. Some of the more notable stronger presidents would be George Washington, Thomas Jefferson, James Madison, Abraham Lincoln, Franklin Delano Roosevelt, and Ronald Reagan. According to Beschloss, there were weak presidents including: 1) John Tyler; 2)Martin Van Buren; 3) Zachary Taylor; 4) Millard Fillmore; 5) Franklin Pierce and 6) William Henry Harrison.[116] Beschloss also states, "For the next quarter-century, with the exception of James Polk, who pursued American expansion and revived the independent treasury, the candlepower of the presidency dimmed…"[117] He also goes on to state, "Few historians would disagree that Abraham Lincoln was our greatest president. What better demonstration could there be of the American idea that anyone can become president than a boy who sprang from the short and simple annals of the poor…"[118] After Polk, Beschloss felt the downfall of America began? Well, in my opinion, the presidents after Polk we were weak and unstable, leading to an unstable infrastructure within the government and in society. However, then came along Abraham Lincoln, who was considered one of the best leaders of this country. He freed the slaves from slavery in the south. He tried to hold the union together throughout the Civil War Era. His administration was the turning point in the United States. After Lincoln, came industrialization and expansion of land, discoveries, inventions and innovations. In some ways the American presidents mirror the Roman rulers. However, there are still many differences in the leadership styles of both Ancient Rome and America.

Abraham Lincoln, The president who saved an Empire Abraham Lincoln's Second Inaugural Address Given on Saturday, March 4, 1865

Fellow-Countrymen:

At this second appearing to take the oath of the Presidential office there is less occasion for an extended address than there was at the first. Then a statement somewhat in detail of a course to be pursued seemed fitting and proper. Now, at the expiration of four years, during which public declarations have been constantly called forth on every point and phase of the great contest which still absorbs the attention and engrosses the energies of the nation, little that is new could be presented. The progress of our arms, upon which all else chiefly depends, is as well known to the public as to myself, and it is, I trust, reasonably satisfactory and encouraging to all. With high hope for the future, no prediction in regard to it is ventured.

On the occasion corresponding to this four years ago all thoughts were anxiously directed to an impending civil war. All dreaded it, all sought to avert it. While the inaugural address was being delivered from this place, devoted altogether to 'saving' the Union without war, urgent agents were in the city seeking to 'destroy' it without war— seeking to dissolve the Union and divide effects by negotiation. Both party's deprecated war, but one of them would 'make' war rather than let the nation survive, and the other would 'accept' war rather than let it perish, and the war came.

One-eighth of the whole population were colored slaves, not distributed generally over the Union, but localized in the southern part of it. These slaves constituted a peculiar and powerful interest. All knew that this interest was somehow the cause of the war. To strengthen, perpetuate, and extend this interest was the object for which the insurgents would rend the Union even by war, while the Government claimed no right to do more than to restrict the territorial enlargement of it. Neither party expected for the war the magnitude or the duration, which it has already attained. Neither anticipated that the 'cause' of the conflict might cease with or even before the conflict itself should cease. Each looked for an easier triumph, and a result less fundamental and astounding. Both read the same Bible and pray to the same God, and each invokes His aid against the other. It may seem strange that any men should dare to ask a just God's assistance in wringing their bread from the sweat of other men's faces, but let us judge not, that we be not judged. The prayers of both could not be answered. That of neither has been answered fully. The Almighty has His own purposes. "Woe unto the world because of offenses; for it must needs be that offenses come, but woe to that man by whom the offense cometh." If we shall suppose that American slavery is one of those offenses which, in the providence of God, must needs come, but which, having continued through His appointed time, He now wills to remove, and that He gives to both North and South this terrible war as the woe due to those by whom the offense came, shall we discern therein any departure from those divine attributes which the believers in a living God always ascribe to Him? Fondly do we hope, fervently do we pray, that this mighty scourge of war may speedily pass away. Yet, if God wills that it continue until all the wealth piled by the bondsman's two hundred and fifty years of unrequited toil shall be sunk, and until every drop of blood drawn with the lash shall be paid by another drawn with the sword, as was said three thousand years ago, so still it must be said "the judgments of the Lord are true and righteous altogether."

    With malice toward none, with charity for all, with firmness in the right as God gives us to see the right, let us strive on to finish the work we are in, to bind up the nation's wounds, to care for him who shall have borne the battle and for his widow and his orphan, to do all which may achieve and cherish a just and lasting peace among ourselves and with all nations.

Source Information:
www.infoplease.com
Abraham Lincoln's Second Inaugural Address

Part 7
The Year 1968: The American and European, "Counter Cultural Decline"

The year 1968 will forever be known as the year that world changed. In the eyes of many, 1968 is the year the world transformed. In the 1968 and the years following America was noted for its protests, economic problems, cultural changes and politics. The Vietnam War was one of the major factors in not only American history but also world history. In the year 1968 the emergence of the media became a strong element of societal change. For example the media broadcasted the Vietnam War and Tet Offensive on TV, showing the people of American and around the world the violence and destruction of war. After 1968, people of America had a hard time trusting their government. Trusting the U.S. government was never the same after this point. The people rebelled against the government in a period of societal and cultural change noted to all Americans as the Counter-Cultural Revolution. This revolution started in the 1960's and lasted until the early 1980's. Across the world, 1968 was a time of upheaval, protest and societal change.

It left its mark on both Capitalism and Communism. The Communist ideology never rebounded after the changing times of the 1960's and 1970's. It died out at the end of the 1980's with the fall of the Soviet Union. The Capitalist economy was also hit hard by bad economic times with periods of stagflation and recession in the 1970's and an oil price hike in the late 1970's. The capitalist economy would somewhat rebound in the 1980's and become more powerful in the 1990's under the strong economic times of President Bill Clinton.

The year 1968 led to major economic problems and high unemployment rates around the world, especially in the America, Europe and Russia. High unemployment rates led to major strikes, protests, marches against the government and the Vietnam War. Lack of consumer knowledge and spending led to a period of stagflation and depression in the stock markets. The Depression / Stagflation era of the 1970's was not as bad as the one in the 1930's but it had profound effect on the society and the beliefs of the people, especially in America. Rising oil prices led to disbelief among consumers.

The Counter Cultural Revolution was a period of change in the societal structure, especially in America. It was a time of people trying new things such as sexual relations in public, drugs and other rebellious things. This period of the Counter Cultural Revolution was a societal movement or revolution which led to more conservatism rather than liberalism in the environment and in the government. By the middle of 1968 this movement spurred many radical movements across the United States and around the world. The movements were for women's rights, affirmative action, abortion rights and Civil Rights. That was a few of the many radical movements that took place between 1968 and the mid to late1970's. It was the start of a new wave of music called, "Rock n Roll." It was the era of the polyester suit, platform shoes, famous nightclubs and disco music. Americans were tired of being told what to do and how to do it. Around the world groups like this were emerging as well. According to the book, 1968: The World Transformed, there are four ways to understand the significance of the changes the occurred in 1968.

First, the events of 1968 unfolded at a very important time in the Cold War. Also according to the book, the long rivalry between the two superpowers created a link between domestic and international affairs, social and cultural developments and world politics. Therefore, according to the book, a complex set of relationships existed in the international system and shifts on the local, national and global level led to resonation between the two superpowers.[119]

Secondly, the book suggests that 1968 was a global phenomenon because of mass media. The types of media used, according to the book, were television, radio and movies. The media was a powerful influence during the time and became instruments of social movement, which in the future created cultural and transnational linkages all over the world, especially during the Vietnam War.[120]

Thirdly, the book continues on by saying that activists throughout the world operated as part of formal and informal networks for communication and collaboration purposes. Therefore, the book suggests that 1968 was a global phenomenon when dealing with cooperation among protest movements and protest groups in various countries. As it was stated this period in history was most talked about because of the amounts of protests, sit-downs, strikes and movements.[121]

Fourth, the book talks about 1968 being a global phenomenon because the protagonists believed in the same common cause: They struggled in opposition to the domestic and international status quo in the East and West and in the North and South as well.[122] In the west, they fought against social repression and discrimination of minority groups and in the east, the fought against authoritarian governments and for liberal democracy.[123]

One of the major causes of unrest in 1968 through the 1970's was the Vietnam War. The media played a big role in bringing the war to the American people. Other major causes of unrest were the fight against discrimination for blacks and the fight for women's equality. This would bring about lots of protests and strikes, dealing with abortion rights and Affirmative Action. Also during this era four major important leaders were killed or assassinated including one president of the United States, John F Kennedy was assassinated on Nov. 22, 1963 in Dallas, Texas. His brother Robert F. Kennedy was later assassinated after the California Primary in 1968 and two leaders of the black movement Malcolm X and Martin Luther King Jr. were killed in 1968. All these killings were due in part causes to the counter cultural revolution growing so strong in America. As for problems overseas, the Chinese Cultural Revolution caused an upheaval in China leading to protests for freedom under Mao Zedong, attacks on elite institutions, not only at

Berkley and Columbia in America, but at the University of Paris and other country universities and Czech leader Dubcek threatened the Warsaw Pact with liberalism of the press, movies and television angering the Soviet Union which would later lead to an overthrow and reinstatement due to lack of potential leaders. Americans also feared the spreading of Communism all over Europe in a period known as the "Red Scare" from the 1950's through the 1970's. Both the Soviets and Americans were in hard economic times during the 1970's and it was compounded with the new computer revolution of the 1980's, which was part of the demise of the Soviet Union and Communist ideal.

Modern Society was shaped in many ways from the year 1968. This could be considered to be the age of extremes. There are many differences and similarities between the year of 1968 and today. Society today was affected by 1968 in a negative way when we consider family. We see single parent families and a high divorce rate. The family is not the same institution it used to be in the 1940's and 1950's. Togetherness and tradition has not been part of the family since this time. The famed baby boom generation of the 1970's led to problems such as AIDS and other sexually transmitted diseases, high infant death, high child abuse, high spousal abuse cases and high divorce rates. The conservative revolution worries more about the military and rich more than liberal values of the family as an institution of life.

Society has also changed when it comes to media getting involved in political matters and wartime matters. Other ways society has changed due to the influences of 1968 are the increase in number of poor people in the street and the shrinking middle class. There is more stress being put on military spending, buying more military equipment and the increasing power of the personal computer. There is an increased focus on the expansion of the internet superhighway and the use of computers in wartime efforts. Two of the most important concepts that we still see today in society, due to the revolution era of 1968, are affirmative action and abortion.

In conclusion, we can see that 1968 has had a profound effect in society, not only in America but also in the former Soviet Republics and in Europe. Also, we can see a profound effect on how society in today's culture and tradition follows the way of the conservatism rather than liberalism due to radical movements spurred by the counter cultural revolution. We can see problems and chaos in economics, politics, the institution of the family and social issues such as affirmative action and abortion.

Chapter 3
Society and Economics in Rome and America

The Socio-Economic System and How it was a cause of decline in Rome and America

There was about all the Romans a heroic tone peculiar to ancient life. Their virtues were great and noble, and these virtues made them great and noble. They possessed a natural majesty that was not put on and taken off at pleasure, as was that of certain eastern monarchs when they put on or took off their garments of Tyrian dye. It is hoped that this is not wholly lost from the world, although the sense of earthly vanity inculcated by Christianity may have swallowed it up in humility.

Herman Melville (1819-1891)
The Piazza Tales and Other Prose Pieces 1839-1860,
The Writings of Herman Melville, vol. 9
Columbia World of Quotations (1996)

Parts 1 – 4
Roman Socio-Economic Policy

Our own country furnishes antiquities as ancient and durable, and as useful, as any; rocks at least as well covered with lichens, and a soil, which, if it is virgin, is, but virgin mould, the very dust of nature. What if we cannot read Rome or Greece, Etruria or Carthage, or Egypt or Babylon, on these; are our cliffs bare?

Henry David Thoreau (1817–1862), U.S. philosopher, author, naturalist
A Week on the Concord and Merrimack Rivers (1849)
The Writings of Henry David Thoreau, vol. 1, p. 265, Houghton Mifflin (1906)

John F. Kennedy's Inaugural Address
Given on Friday, January 20, 1961

Vice President Johnson, Mr. Speaker, Mr. Chief Justice, President Eisenhower, Vice President Nixon, President Truman, and Reverend Clergy, fellow citizens:

We observe today not a victory of party but a celebration of freedom—symbolizing an end as well as a beginning—signifying renewal as well as change. For I have sworn before you and Almighty God the same solemn oath our forebears prescribed nearly a century and three-quarters ago.

The world is very different now. For man holds in his mortal hands the power to abolish all forms of human poverty and all forms of human life. And yet the same revolutionary beliefs for which our forebears fought are still at issue around the globe—the belief that the rights of man come not from the generosity of the state, but from the hand of God.

We dare not forget today that we are the heirs of that first revolution. Let the word go forth from this time and place, to friend and foe alike, that the torch has been passed to a new generation of Americans—born in this century, tempered by war, disciplined by a hard and bitter peace, proud of our ancient heritage—and unwilling to witness or permit the slow undoing of those human rights to which this Nation has always been committed, and to which we are committed today at home and around the world.

Let every nation know, whether it wishes us well or ill, that we shall pay any price, bear any burden, meet any hardship, support any friend, oppose any foe, in order to assure the survival and the success of liberty. This much we pledge—and more

    To those old allies whose cultural and spiritual origins we share, we pledge the loyalty of faithful friends. United, there is little we cannot do in a host of cooperative ventures. Divided, there is little we can do—for we dare not meet a powerful challenge at odds and split asunder.

    To those new States whom we welcome to the ranks of the free, we pledge our word that one form of colonial control shall not have passed away merely to be replaced by a far more iron tyranny. We shall not always expect to find them supporting our view. But we shall always hope to find them strongly supporting their own freedom—and to remember that, in the past, those who foolishly sought power by riding the back of the tiger ended up inside.

To those peoples in the huts and villages across the globe struggling to break the bonds of mass misery, we pledge our best efforts to help them help themselves, for whatever period is required—not because the Communists may be doing it, not because we seek their votes, but because it is right. If a free society cannot help the many who are poor, it cannot save the few who are rich.

To our sister republics south of our border, we offer a special pledge—to convert our good words into good deeds—in a new alliance for progress—to assist free men and free governments in casting off the chains of poverty. But this peaceful revolution of hope cannot become the prey of hostile powers. Let all our neighbors know that we shall join with them to oppose aggression or subversion anywhere in the Americas. And let every other power know that this Hemisphere intends to remain the master of its own house.

To that world assembly of sovereign states, the United Nations, our last best hope in an age where the instruments of war have far outpaced the instruments of peace, we renew our pledge of support—to prevent it from becoming merely a forum for invective—to strengthen its shield of the new and the weak—and to enlarge the area in which its writ may run.

Finally, to those nations who would make themselves our adversary, we offer not a pledge but a request: that both sides begin anew the quest for peace, before the dark powers of destruction unleashed by science engulf all humanity in planned or accidental self-destruction.

We dare not tempt them with weakness. For only when our arms are sufficient beyond doubt can we be certain beyond doubt that they will never be employed.

But neither can two great and powerful groups of nations take comfort from our present course—both sides overburdened by the cost of modern weapons, both rightly alarmed by the steady spread of the deadly atom, yet both racing to alter that uncertain balance of terror that stays the hand of mankind's final war.

So let us begin anew—remembering on both sides that civility is not a sign of weakness, and sincerity is always subject to proof. Let us never negotiate out of fear. But let us never fear to negotiate.
Let both sides explore what problems unite us instead of belaboring those problems, which divide us.

Let both sides, for the first time, formulate serious and precise proposals for the inspection and control of arms—and bring the absolute power to destroy other nations under the absolute control of all nations.

Let both sides seek to invoke the wonders of science instead of its terrors. Together let us explore the stars, conquer the deserts, eradicate disease, tap the ocean depths, and encourage the arts and commerce.

Let both sides unite to heed in all corners of the earth the command of Isaiah—to "undo the heavy burdens...and to let the oppressed go free."

And if a beachhead of cooperation may push back the jungle of suspicion, let both sides join in creating a new endeavor, not a new balance of power, but a new world of law, where the strong are just and the weak secure and the peace preserved.

All this will not be finished in the first 100 days. Nor will it be finished in the first 1,000 days, nor in the life of this Administration, nor even perhaps in our lifetime on this planet. But let us begin.

In your hands, my fellow citizens, more than in mine, will rest the final success or failure of our course. Since this country was founded, each generation of Americans has been summoned to give testimony to its national loyalty. The graves of young Americans who answered the call to service surround the globe.

Now the trumpet summons us again—not as a call to bear arms, though arms we need; not as a call to battle, though embattled we are—but a call to bear the burden of a long twilight struggle, year in and year out, "rejoicing in hope, patient in tribulation"—a struggle against the common enemies of man: tyranny, poverty, disease, and war itself.

Can we forge against these enemies a grand and global alliance, North and South, East and West that can assure a more fruitful life for all mankind? Will you join in that historic effort?

In the long history of the world, only a few generations have been granted the role of defending freedom in its hour of maximum danger. I do not shrink from this responsibility—I welcome it. I do not believe that any of us would exchange places with any other people or any other generation. The energy, the faith, the devotion which we bring to this endeavor will light our country and all who serve it—and the glow from that fire can truly light the world. A

And so, my fellow Americans: ask not what your country can do for you—ask what you can do for your country.

My fellow citizens of the world: ask not what America will do for you, but what together we can do for the freedom of man.

Finally, whether you are citizens of America or citizens of the world, ask of us the same high standards of strength and sacrifice which we ask of you. With a good conscience our only sure reward, with history the final judge of our deeds, let us go forth to lead the land we love, asking His blessing and His help, but knowing that here on earth God's work must truly be our own.

Source Information:
www.infoplease.com
John F. Kennedy Inaugural Address

Part 1
Overview of Roman Social and Economic Life

The three most important things in the life of an empire are geography, politics and socio-economic life. Rome, at one point in their empire, had a balance of all three functions. This chapter will discuss how the Roman people lived their lives. The mentality of the Roman people throughout the course of the empire changed with the evolution of the times. The people and the society of Rome adapted to the times as well as any empire in world history. The people also wanted to make changes in their society with the inventions and innovative ideas of certain Roman individuals. The evolution of art, architecture, philosophy, inventions, discoveries and politics / economics had a major effect on the people of Rome. Romans had their leisure time and their entertainment just like the Americans of today. Gladiatorial combat was one of the major forms of entertainment. Outside the politics and economics of Rome, people had a lifestyle and people had a way of life with different customs, cultures and ideas.

Rome placed importance on the armies that protected the country's boundaries. Rome had a strong defense and strategic planning setup against their outside foes. The armies were strong and their generals were noble and knowledgeable. Their armies were built as a legion of brothers and they would fight and conquer and expand the Roman Empire. The Roman people were a war-like people who liked the sight of death and blood.

    The Roman people loved their art and architecture. Their art is remembered in today's culture in Europe and the United States. The use of the column and the use of marble could be looked at as a Roman trait. The people of Rome loved to create. Many artifacts show us that Rome was a majestic place to live and learn. Some of the ancient Roman buildings still stand in Rome today as a memory of the leaders and the people that have gone before them. These buildings are of course weathered and falling apart but they are still around for generations to see and learn. Art is the same with the many Italian artists that came after the Roman Empire. Art and architecture made Rome beautiful and memorable. Some of those Italians came to America as immigrants to bring of the art and architecture. For example, the Italians painted the train stations in New York City. They also helped in the architecture of buildings in New York City. One of the more famous Italians to be recognized was the founder of the New World Christopher Columbus. He is recognized in Columbus Square with a statue.

    People's everyday life in Rome consisted of farming, planting, writing books, art, architecture, trading, fishing, building and making a living working in a profession of choice. Family life in Rome according to F.R. Cowell, is more holy and religious than anything else in society. He states, "There is nothing more holy, nothing more securely guarded by every religious instinct than each individual Roman's home."[124] He goes on to say that the Roman people are dignified, serious-folk deserving respect rather than affection. Cowell uses Marcus Aurelius as an example, by stating that this emperor said there was no word in Latin to express the tender affectionate love of parents to their children.[125] Women during this time were usually looked at as the home-bearers and were never considered to be leaders or heirs to the Roman throne after a Roman ruler died or left the throne. The Romans always encouraged large families. Why would they want big families? The boys, when they grew up, were either farmers, members of the Roman legion armies, or made to fight for entertainment in gladiatorial combat, especially if they were part of the minority in Roman Society. The girls were the home bearers and the child-raisers, not really having particular function in the Roman way of life besides those features. Big families were important during the time to preserve the family name.

    The Romans had their leisure time also. There were shows and spectacles for entertainment. There were the theatres and amphitheatres. There were the Races and the bloody events in the Coliseum. People paid to see this entertainment as a way of boosting the economy of the empire. People walked a lot in Rome and they also went to relax at the outdoor baths that were built for their leisure. It was more or less like American society today, but with more restriction.

    Economically, the Romans were balanced and strong for a number of years. The rulers of the Roman Empire kept a close eye on the economy of the empire for many reasons including the building up of the Roman legion and its armies, the expansion and imperialization of new territories surrounding the empire and to keep massive population of Rome was happy and entertained. Lots of the money that made up Rome's economy came from taxes and tourism. People from the early days of history had to pay their taxes to the state. These taxes made up about 75% of the empire economy and also increased throughout the years because of the art and architectural revolution during these times. Architecture of from the center of the Roman Empire, the building of residential housing and means of entertainment for the Roman people also added to the beauty and economy of Rome.

According to a 1997 article in the USA Today, Richard Vedder, a well-known column writer, wrote about the Roman Empire's economy, "Ancient Rome did not become relatively rich through capital formation and technological advances, the usual causes of economic progress... As a government center it thrived in living largely off the tribute (which was the Latin word for taxes) of the provinces and conquered lands."[126] In other words, as the Roman Empire expanded throughout Europe, the conquered land's people had to pay taxes to the Roman Government making it increasingly easy to be a power economically in the ancient world.

A good economy led to good social structure in the Roman Empire. With money being made through out Rome, because of the residents of the Rome and their work ethic. Rome expanded and flourished and was considered the light of the world. Vedder goes on to say about the economy of Rome, "Rome did not produce most of its wealth...prosperity came at the expense of individuals in the conquered lands of Spain, France, Northern Africa (Carthage), etc."[127] This fact, according to Vedder, was the reason why Rome failed and declined. Without the support of the conquered lands, Rome was not much of an economic power and without that money they would not have been as strong as it was. The strength of the Roman legions and the Roman armies allowed Rome to flourish and prosper.

    The introduction of Christianity was also said to be a reason for decline in Rome. Christianity, during the time of the ruler Constantine, was first introduced and later flourished throughout Rome. Christianity eventually split the Roman Empire into two parts. The social structure changed and the people were confused. The strength and power of the Roman legion was no more. Christianity was a major reason of the fall of Rome. Years after the Roman Empire, the Holy Roman Empire introduced the Vatican and Papacy as a source of power and control in Rome. There were now two leaders. One of the religious world and one of the political world.

    So was it the social and economic structures of Rome that caused it to fall? Well, yes it was. More than the leadership and geography of Rome, the social structure and economic structure had more effect on the decline and fall of Rome. The evolution of the empire got to the minds of the Roman people and the people were confused.

The confusion led to uprisings and civil war, which eventually led to the downfall of a once great power.

Part 2
Roman Architecture And Art: A Source of Economic Power and Strength

Rome was noted for its architectural beauty and its works of art. Both architecture and art were a main source of income for the Roman Republic. Rome was beautiful in its, architecture, due to the decadence of marble and stone. The center of Rome was the highlight with numerous buildings, structures and government fortresses. Rome's architecture can still be seen today in Rome and some of the ideas and thoughts were funneled into America during the time of immigration in the late 1800's / early 1900's. Rome's people took up numerous trades and occupations to build up their capital city. These people are the early engineers of world history. They were engineers, construction workers, architects and laborers. It took thousands of these people to build up Rome. Because of their lack of transportation on land, these men had to work by foot, carrying and handling these building materials all over the center of Rome. Parts of Roman fortresses are still seen today. The Coliseum, site of the gladiatorial combat, still stands today, weathered and torn, but still standing in the center of Rome. The beauty and light of Rome can still be seen in its grandeur. Throughout history, people have been visiting these historical places to learn more about the times.

The artists and sculptors are also remembered today in museums throughout the world. People that brought the world the art revolution came mostly during the Renaissance era of Italy, but we can see evidence of art and sculpture in the ancient Roman Times. The making of statues in honor of the fallen generals, rulers and famous people of Roman history live on throughout history. The Coliseum was a combination of both sculpture and architecture. Sculptures and art could be seen built around and inside the confines of this huge arena.

In the next couple of subsections of this part we will look at some major pieces of architecture and art in Italy during the Roman Empire. We will discuss its impact on the empire socially and economically.

2.1 The Coliseum

The Coliseum was noted as one of the most notable architectural masterpieces of the Roman Empire, which is still standing today. Being all weather beaten and torn in Italy today, it still stands as an icon for yesteryear. According to the Frommer's, "Guide to Past and Present Rome", The Coliseum was known as a "Flavian Amphitheater," which was built in the middle of the broad valley between the Palatine, Caelian and Esquiline hills.[128] As we know from the first chapter, geography played a huge role in the dynamics of Rome. The center of Rome could be found amongst the hills and valleys giving it ample protection from outsiders. It also would bring an element of surprise to people as well. The ruler Vespasian started the project of building the

Coliseum shortly after 70 AD and Titus first opened the Coliseum ten years later.[129] According to the Frommer's Guide, the dynamics of the Coliseum were unprecedented for its time.

"....The major axis of its elliptical plan is 188m long, the minor axis attains 156m and the walls in the outer ring rise to almost 50m above the ground; more than 100,000 cubic meters of travertine were used to build it and even the metal pins that held the blocks together must have weighed more than 300 tons..."[130]

The interior of the Coliseum is just as beautiful and interesting as the exterior. It leads to the question: How did the Romans build this huge amphitheater by hand and foot? The answer would probably be their nationalism toward their country and their determination and diligence to get it finished. The Romans were hard and diligent workers, which led to a better economic and social structure in the empire. According to the Frommer's Guide, the interior of the Coliseum was also unprecedented for its time built with columns, corridors and a basement floor. According to Connolly's book, The Ancient City: Life of Classical Athens and Rome, it is said that the Coliseum was built out of concrete which was about 12 m deep. The concrete was partly laid in clay and partly retained by brick-face walls.[131]

"....The eighty arches at ground level were progressively numbered (the number corresponding to that on the spectator's tessera or admission card) and led, via a system of internal corridors, to the 160 outlets that took *the visitor to his place on the steps of the Cavea, which was borne up by arches and vaults…"*[132]

Other internal dimensions, According to the Frommer's Guide, include a wooden floor bearing a layer of sand and covering the area of about 76m by 46m. The stands were subdivided into three sections. Each sector of the stands or Cavea (in Latin) was reserved for a particular class of individuals, the places on top being assigned to the poor or the least important people, most notably the minorities of the time. Also including the people standing in the arena, the total capacity of the amphitheater was 70,000 people.[133]

These people would pay to see death and blood on the floor of the Coliseum through gladiatorial combat, wild beast hunts and many other events, which were held in the confines of the building. It was for entertainment and the people enjoyed it. The Romans, compared to the Spartans of Greece, were the most aggressive, warlike people of the era. These people loved blood, death and destruction. That is what the Romans paid for in the Coliseum. This incidentally was also part of the massive economic income of Rome. The amphitheater payments made up about 25% of Rome's economy. It was definitely a moneymaker in the minds of the Roman ruler, therefore, they continued the carnage of death. Naval battles would also take place within the Coliseum, by filling the center of the Coliseum up with water and recreating ship structures. According to Frommer's Guide, the last and final show that was held in the Coliseum came in 523 AD under the ruler Theodoric, "The King of the Ostrogoths" (after the Roman Empire declined). Gladiatorial combat was abolished in 438 AD, a few years after the death of the empire.[134] Under the ruler of Domitian, after it was decided not to have naval battles anymore, a series of passages and rooms were built underneath the floor of the arena. According to Frommer's Guide, "These underground rooms contained facilities and stored the stage equipment (meaning the weapons of death) such as the scenery used in the hunts…"[135] The underground consisted of animal routes for the wild animals used in the hunt scenes, skylights, elevators and cells for the gladiators. The elevators would bring the animals and gladiators to the floor of the arena and the animal and gladiator would battle to the death.

    The Coliseum, was truly huge and beautiful piece of architecture that led to the social and economic structure of the Ancient Roman Empire. The Coliseum was the centerpiece of the Roman Culture and the Roman Ideal. It still stands today in all its grandeur, but the people of today lack the knowledge of the history and nationalistic belief of the ancient Roman Era. The building was the center of the culture of death and blood and still today it is looked at as a great piece of architecture. According to The Ancient City: Life of Classical Athens & Rome, only the northern portion of the building still stands today. Also according to this book, after it was seriously damaged in an earthquake in the ninth century, it was pillaged for building materials.[136]

2.2 The Great Square of the Coliseum

These buildings and sculptures surrounded the Coliseum walls and made the massive building look even more beautiful. As people walked towards the Coliseum, they walked through a series of buildings and sculptures. One of the most obvious of these sculptures stood right beside the Coliseum. The Colossus of Nero: This was a giant, bronze statue of the emperor Nero, which stood 30m high and which was a work created by Greek sculptor named Zenodoros.[137] Other notable buildings and sculptures in this area include The Temple of Venus and Rome, which was a building designed by ruler Hadrian. This building, according to Frommer's Guide, was dedicated to the divine ancestress of the Julian Family and was inaugurated in 135 AD, and then reconstructed in 310 AD, after a fire destroyed it, by Maxentius.[138] The Meta Sudans: meaning the "turn of sweat", was found at the beginning of the road that leads to the Coliseum. This was a fountain built in the middle of the 1st century, which had a shape like one of the "Metae," also known as, turning points in the Circus that chariots had to race around.[139] The final monument or sculpture found in this area was called The Arch of Constantine: which was erected in 312 AD by the Senate and the People of Rome in honor of the late Emperor Constantine who had liberated the city and the state from the "tyrant" Maxentius during his victory in the battle of the Milvian Bridge. He also was remembered for introducing Christianity to the empire, which eventually led to its demise in the 4th century.[140]

These monuments made the outside of the Coliseum look just as glorious as the inside of the building. They are also a remembrance of fallen Roman rulers that were heroes of the time and today looked at as murderers, tyrants and imperialists.

2.3 The Forum Romanum

The Forum Romanum is known today as the Ancient Roman Forum, which was the basic area of the Roman Government governing from the center of Rome. The Forum Romanum was made up of fifteen buildings at the time of Augustus, the first Roman Emperor of the republic. This area was noted as the commercial, religious, political and legal center of the city. This was an ancient version of the White House and Washington D.C. in the United States. It is the Romans' layout that was never matched in beauty and grandeur until the United States got its independence and created Washington D.C. in the likeness and eyes of the Roman structure. The architecture of this area made Rome the powerhouse of its time. The architecture was unprecedented in the history of engineering, science and construction and they did it all by hand and foot. The lack of technology made it hard to build these areas up, but because of the diligent work ethic, the Romans never gave up until the work was done.

The Forum Romanum was an area made up of fifteen buildings. The valley of the Forum, which was found between two hills Palatine and Viminal, was noted as a burial ground for fallen rulers, famous people and army troops. This could be a parallel idea to the Arlington National Cemetery in Washington D.C. The Forum Romanum was the beginning of the glory and light of Rome.

The fifteen buildings are as follows: 1) The Tabularium: which is noted as the state archive of Rome (Library), provided a monumental backdrop to the square.[141] The idea parallel to the Library of Congress in Washington D.C.; 2) The Temple of Concord: which was built up against the Tabularium, was built in memory of Marcus Furius Camillus, who was said to have had it built in 367 BC to commemorate the peace settlement between the Patricians and the Plebians (Rich vs. Poor uprisings). The idea is parallel to either the class of economics in

America or Karl Marx's the Bourgeoisie vs. the Proletariat (Businessmen vs. Worker Uprisings);[142] 3) The Temple of Saturn: was noted to be one of the most ancient shrines in Ancient Rome and was begun during the last years of the kings. It was inaugurated at the beginning of the republic in 498 AD. Its huge base was supposed to be used for the state treasury called the Aerarium, but because of a fire it was unable to hold that function in the structure of government.[143] The idea is parallel to the Department of the Treasury building in Washington D.C.; 4) The Basilica Julia: The most common function of the basilica was its use as a courthouse. The Basilica Julia housed the court of the Centumviri (literally, one hundred men, although the number was actually one hundred eighty). Often the one hundred eighty jurors were divided up into four groups of forty-five, separated by screens or curtains.[144] This building was used as a Supreme Court type building for the Romans and it parallels the United States Supreme Court building in Washington D.C. It was later used as a holy, religious place; 5) The Rostra: The Rostra is the name of the great speaker's platform in the Forum, where speakers addressed crowds. This platform marks many of the great and famous speeches in Roman history.[145] Julius Caesar later removed this platform. This platform parallels the speaker's platforms on the House and Senate floors in the Capitol building.; 6) The Temple of Castor and Pollux: is named after the twin sons of Jupiter in Greek mythology. According to the Forum Romanum website:

"Legend has it that during the battle of Lake Regillus two youths on horseback, far excelling mortals in beauty of form and features, appeared to Postumius, the Roman leader and charged at the head of the Roman cavalry... They wounded all they met with their spears, and drove the Latins before them, putting them to flight, taking their camp, and ending the battle. A little later, according to legend, two youths appeared in the same manner in the Roman Forum at sunset. They were attired in military uniform, were very tall and beautiful and of the same age, both looked as if they had just come from battle. Even their horses were tired from the battle. They dismounted, and washed in the fountain near the temple of Vesta. In answer to the many questions of people who were standing about, eager to know whether the strangers had brought news from the camp, they announced the Roman victory and related the particulars of the battle. The story goes that after they had left the Forum they were never seen again, despite efforts of the magistrate of the city."[146]

Three massive columns remain from the Temple of Castor and Pollux. They are over forty-eight feet high. The temple had been rebuilt between 7 B.C. and 6 A.D. The statues of Castor and Pollux can be seen at the top of the stairs of the Capitoline Hill.[147] This parallels the Lincoln Memorial which is in view of the Capitol building in Washington D.C.; 7) The Temple of Divus Julius: In 31 BC Octavian, Caesar's adoptive son, built this temple in two years (29BC) and dedicated it to the deified Caesar, Divus Julius. Some researchers say that it was built on the spot where Julius Caesar's dead body was burned after his assassination.[148]

This, in some ways, parallels the tomb of ex-slain president John F. Kennedy with the "eternal flame," which sits in front of the grave and gives off a sense of immortality or "eternal life."; 8) The Temple of Vesta: This building was found in the center of the Forum Romanum.[149] It was built round, imitating the primitive round huts in which the Latins had lived. The priestesses of Vesta, the Vestal Virgins, lived in a sacred residence immediately next to the temple. The section of the temple, which stands today, was reconstructed in 1930.[150] This could mimic the round home of Thomas Jefferson called Monticello and was later made into a memorial in Washington D.C. in honor of the father of freedom and the Declaration of Independence; 9) The Regia: The Regia means "royal palace" in Latin. This Royal Palace was found to the south of House of Vestals and traditionally thought to be the residence of King Numa. Later, ruler Augustus Caesar donated the Regia, to the Vestals.[151] The Regia is similar to the moving of the capital cities in the United States in the 1800s. The capital was in Philadelphia before Washington D.C. was created, which is how the royal palace acted as a White House type building; 10) The Basilica Aemilia: The purpose of this Basilica was to provide visitors to the Forum with a comfortable and sheltered place where they can work on specific functions that were normally done in an open place. These functions include the administration of justice and business.[152] This is the same as a hotel for the tourists to stay in while visiting. Hotels have conference rooms for business purposes. The Basilica Aemilia was an ancient hotel in the center of the administrative district in Rome just like hotels surround Washington D.C. for pending business people and dignitaries; 11) The Curia: The curia was constructed by the Ancient Romans for meetings and deliberations of the Senate and The Comitium which was constructed for the assemblies of the people.[153] This mimics the legislative branch of the of the United States, where Congress and the House of Representatives are located in the same Capitol building to deliberate matters of the American people; 12) The Temple of Venus Genetrix: Which was one of the only buildings in the Forum Romanum to be built with certain design because it was built for Julius Caesar himself. It was named after Venus because this Greek god was considered highly in the family of Julius Caesar.[154] This is similar to monuments built commemorating rulers including the Washington Monument in Washington D.C.; 13) Temple of Augustus: The first ruler of Rome built this temple in his name. This is the place he would govern from throughout his reign as emperor of Rome.[155] 14) The Forum of Caesar: The building was built in the time of Julius Caesar. He, along with the eleven others in the Caesar tradition would govern from this spot in the center of the Forum Romanum.[156] 15) The Temple of Mars Ultor: This is another temple named after a Greek god and found within the confines of the Forum Romanum. Roman people tended to follow stories about the Greeks and Greek mythology from time to time, because they were their ancient successors and the Romans learned a lot from the Greek philosophers.

2.4 Conclusion

When looking at certain Roman architecture and art we can see the social and economic importance to the Roman Empire. Roman architecture may be said to be cost insufficient. In order to build Rome's architecture of grandeur, the Roman government sought out ways to allocate money to construct these buildings. The source of the money originated from the empire's tax system. Economically speaking, the tax money could have been utilized to strengthen their army or provide more for their people. Instead, these buildings were essential means for the rulers to exercise their power. The Roman rulers took great pride in building arches and temples, which commemorated their ruling period. Considering the financial implications, we may infer that there was a lack of money to construct an abundance of the temples, arches and buildings, which rendered a lack of resources for its people. As for the American perspective on architecture and art, we see similarities between the United States and Rome. One being, the building structure and the parallels we can make between the two empires. The only difference between the United States and Rome, on this point, is the United States utilizes resources efficiently for the proper use of buildings to suit the majority interest. Rome's focus was more individualistic and self-righteous according to the ruler request for construction.

The Roman Empire's Forum Romanum

Part 3
America's African American Slaves vs. Ancient Rome's Gladiators

Slavery was a major part of both America and Rome during their respective empires. The slave trade differs between the empires because Ancient Romans were meticulous in choosing whom they wanted to serve them based on size and strength. To be a gladiator, you had to be strong and move quickly. The gladiators were slaves to the state. They had no choice but to be used for entertainment. The strength and agility of the gladiator allowed for the longevity of battles. In comparison, the African American population of the United States were slaves since the beginning of the union after the Revolutionary War. African Americans were used as laborers and workers. They earned no money. Before the 1950's with the major court case Brown vs. The Board of Education, African Americans were considered slaves of the state. They finally got their rights in the 1950's and started such concepts as "affirmative action" in the 1960's and 1970's. African Americans were the focus of America since the time the country began. They were never considered equal to the white Caucasians in America and still today African Americans are still fighting to be equal to the white people. Slavery caused the country to split into in the 1860's. The American Civil War between the north and south occurred because of many underlying causes, one of those being the slave trade in the south. The north was totally against slavery and the south was for it. The south broke away from the union, causing conflict and confusion in the once strong United States. Slaves were emancipated after the union defeated the Confederates in the American Civil War. Before this period of time though, rich people, especially presidents of the United States, had African American slaves working for them as laborers and workers for no pay.

1.1 The Life of a gladiator according to Daniel Mannix

The gladiators and African Americans slaves were different in that the gladiators were used for entertainment purposes and the African Americans were used as laborers and workers on the farms and in the factories. To better understand the life of gladiator, we must look at a book written by Daniel P. Mannix called, *"The Way of the Gladiator."* This book explains the life of a gladiator in Rome. It discusses, in graphic terms, how gladiators and animals were forced to entertain the thousands of war-like individuals. Times were hard for the Roman Empire during the time the gladiator games were started. They were used as a mechanism to build up the nationalistic spirits of the people again. This entertainment was also used as an economic boost to the Roman Empire. The emperor at the time was one of the most notable rulers of the century. Nero was a man who loved war, blood and fighting. Nero was the ruler who started these bloody games, to fix a declining economy. The times are described to us in the first paragraph of Mannix's book:

"Nero was emperor and for two weeks the mob had been rioting uncontrolled in the streets of Rome. The economy of the greatest empire that the world had ever seen was coming apart....The cost of maintaining Rome's gigantic armed forces, equipped with the latest catapults, ballistae and fast war galleys, was bleeding the nation white and in addition there were the heavy subsidies that had to paid to the satellite nations dependent on Rome's support. The impoverished government had neither the funds nor the power to stop the riots."[157]

The people of Rome concurred that Nero was a ruler who was a tyrant and lunatic. He enjoyed war and battles. He enjoyed the combat. He enjoyed seeing the death of innocent people, the raping of young women and the death and bloody battle between animals. It was explained by Mannix, that there were special announcements of the games and races in the center of Rome. Mannix also states that during these games, "300 pairs of gladiators would fight to the death and twelve hundred condemned criminals would be eaten by lions."[158] Nero enjoyed role-playing and enjoyed seeing people hunt animals or people hunt down other people or animals hunting other animals. The people of Rome were just as war-like. They would fill the coliseum, which sat up to 385,000 and bet on the gladiators and get drunk while doing it. Mannix's book illustrates the vivid experiences of gladiators in battle.

The people of Rome called these battles and reconstructed wars, "The Games." The games created new jobs according to Mannix, which include: animal trappers, gladiator trainers, horse breeders, shippers, contractors, armorers, stadium attendants, promoters and businessmen. These jobs, according to Mannix, spurred a declining Roman economy.[159] According to Mannix, "To have abolished the games would have thrown so many people out of work that the national economy would have collapsed."[160]

So were the games good or bad in the eyes of other cultures? Well, in a way you can say it was a Franklin Delano Roosevelt tactic to create jobs and spur economic growth and better the income of a struggling nation during the time of Nero. You can also look at it and say, yes, it may be spurring the economy, but its killing millions of innocent people. In this light, Nero could be looked at as an Adolf Hilter type ruler who wanted to exterminate the minorities from the empire. You can say that the gladiator games can be looked at as a Holocaust of the Christians and other minorities in the Roman Empire. For Nero, he was looked at as a tyrant and lunatic. However, was he actually bettering his nation through the creation of jobs and the empire's earned income from the 385,000 people that would pack the stadium every day to watch the games. Nonetheless, these games were in humane and wrong.

Today we see stadiums built for sport, but not the killing kind. We have stadiums for such sports as track and field, football, baseball, soccer, etc. These are all competitive sports, which do not involve killing innocent people. It brings in millions of dollars in revenue each year and it also creates jobs for people who are unemployed. Could the Romans set up competitive sports instead of these gladiatorial combat games? In actuality, the civilization before the Romans, the Greeks had competitive games that were non-fatal. These games would later go on to be called the Olympic games, where people show for their talents without the blood and war. Why did the Romans develop such harsh games for competition? Firstly the Greeks, except for the Spartans, were a passive type people who were philosophers and thinkers, whereas the Romans were more war-like and aggressive. Gladiatorial combat mirrored the Greek games in that it was competitive, but the big difference was that they were non-fatal. It seemed that Nero, wanted to rid the country of minorities. Therefore these games were formed to have the minorities of Rome kill each other rather than the government killing them off. Gladiatorial combat was a way of ridding the Empire of opposition to its policies and laws.

    According to Mannix, the mob existed in the time of the Roman Empire. The games, according to Mannix, were a way to keep the mob quiet. The mob would go to watch the games and this would allow the government to run its daily operations. Otherwise, the mob would try to take over the throne of Rome in coups against the government. Rome under Nero, became a self-centered and arrogant empire. Gambling became a problem as the games became more popular throughout the empire. Mannix states about gladiatorial combat: "The Romans worshiped courage and every Roman liked to picture himself as a rough, tough fighter. In Rome, the "little guy" could identify himself with a successful gladiator as modern fight fan can identify himself with a famous prize fighter."[161] In other words, the people started to look up to these gladiators as if they were role models. The children of Roman families would also look up to the gladiators and see that death and war was okay.

The games would go on under other Roman rulers as well, such as, Domitian and Marcus Aurelius. Marcus Aurelius, the great Roman Emperor and philosopher, stated about gladiatorial combat: "I wouldn't mind the games being so brutal and degrading if only they weren't so damned monotonous."[162] Some of the rulers of Rome were not in favor of the games continuing, but to pacify the crowds and mobs, "The Games" continued.

As was said in earlier paragraphs animals were used a lot in these games to kill off people or other domestic or wild animals. Mannix states about the gathering of the animals for the games:

"You may wonder where the Romans got all the animals they used in the games…Trajan gave one set of games that lasted 122 days during which eleven thousand people and ten thousand animals were killed… Titus had five thousand wild animals and four thousand domestic animals killed during the one-hundred day show to celebrate the opening of the Coliseum."[163]

These are just a few examples of how many animals and people were actually killed during these games under different rulers. In 249 AD, Mannix states from the book Rome and the Romans, by Showerman, that the one thousandth anniversary of the founding of Rome was celebrated by emperor Philip in which massive amounts of animals and individual deaths occurred, including, one thousand pairs of gladiators, hippos, giraffes, elephants, tigers, lions, etc.[164] Was gladiatorial combat right for this empire to base itself on? In the years since the last gladiator games, we see more people dying unrightfully than in any war or any accident in world history. If it was meant to be a mass extermination of minorities it sure did work, according to Mannix's statistics. It made the rulers of the time look like killers and tyrants. The people looked like heretics and the empire looked like a death camp or a mercy field. It was not something the empire wanted to be noted for, but in the grand scheme of things it was and it is looked at as one of the falls of ancient Rome.

1.2 The African Americans Slaves

The slave trade in the United States before the Civil War Era of history was very much existent especially among the rich landowners and some of the presidents of United States. African Americans were looked at as a minority. Minorities, such as with Rome, were normally the poor and destitute. Also, minorities would be people of different origin, color, race or religion. African Americans, since the beginning of America have been persecuted and put down for their color. Such as in Rome, there was a slave trade in which the rich oppressors would go and look for the perfect slaves and purchase them. These people would be sold like animals and treated with little respect. Slavery would split a powerful empire into two parts during the time of the Civil Era: The Confederates of the South and Union Protectors of the North. The south fought for slavery for years, because of the vast farms and plantations in the south. The north opposed slavery and wanted to put an end to it. This would lead to one of the biggest social conflicts in world history.

According to Brian Holden Reid and his book, *"The American Civil War,"* in the 1840s, a pro-slavery ideology grew up in the south. It argued that by comparison with brutality of the industrial urban civilization, paternal rural slavery was a positive good.[165] Also stated, is that after the Compromise of 1850, Kansas was asked by the confederates to enter the union as a slave state. Kansas later entered the War on the side of the Union against slavery. The south also wanted the right to bring its slavery into the huge territory gained from Mexico in the War of 1846-47, which was also put down by the Republican government in Washington D.C.[166]

In some ways the slave trade was the same as that of Rome. One main difference was the African American was not used for entertainment purposes. The American slaves gained some independence in the 1950's and received even more rights in the 1960's and 1970's with the emergence of affirmative action and black rights. Slaves before the Civil War Era were made to be the cleaners, farmers, plantation workers and servants of the white elites of America. Even presidents such as Thomas Jefferson, George Washington and Andrew Jackson had slaves working for them. Thomas Jefferson was even said to have an affair with his slave.

      Slavery, no matter the form, disrespected other human beings rights and degraded the minorities. The American and Roman views on slavery were different because of the evolution of societies throughout history, but they both focused on the same concept of discrimination, hatred toward minorities and hatred toward opposition of belief or value.

Part 4
Through the Eyes of Movies: How America, Art and Literature Perceive Roman Gladiatorial Combat

America, through movies, perceived what it was like during Roman times. Gladiatorial combat was depicted in many of these films throughout history, but none really got to the heart of the matter like the movie "*The Gladiator.*" This film, from 2000, won best picture of the year not only because of the acting and the directing, but also because of the premise. This was the first time people of America actually saw what it would be like to be in the Coliseum fighting for your life. People of America finally saw the bad side of the Roman Empire, which was depicted to them as children as the "Light of the World." This part will discuss how Americans and literature perceived the Roman Empire during the times of the gladiators and how this movie actually brought to light the "Evil Side" of the "Light of the World."

The movie, "*Gladiator*" has many references, which deal primarily with the Keatsian method of thinking. The movie refers to art depicting life and dreams becoming reality. The movie can also be said to have references to Schubert, Melville and Hopkins as well. The Keats poem that is mostly reflected in the movie is "Ode on a Grecian Urn." Robert Browning also uses art to depict life after someone dies. Browning's poem "My Last Duchess" can be said to relate to Maxius's dream in the movie. All these late romantic writers and composers can definitely relate to some of the art, sculptures and structures depicted in the movie. The movie Gladiator had many themes to it, one being that the reality of life after death is not a falsity as seen through the constant dream Maximus continued to have about his dead wife and child.

The idea of art playing a role in this movie is seen in many different ways throughout the film. It's shown through dreams, sculpture, art, structure, fashion and music. This film was one of the best films ever because of its art direction, fashion, wardrobe and score. The music of this film was intense during the war scenes and action scenes and calm and consoling during times of death and betrayal. The fashion and wardrobe depicted the times of the Roman Empire. The fashion can be said to be contradicting most like Hopkins was contradicting in his writings. The rich/the poor, the royalty/slaves, old/young and women/men were all depicted differently. The times had a lot to do with their depictions, but we can also look to Hopkins for answers. One of biggest things we see through Hopkins is a contradiction of different groups of people or objects. To answer these questions of contradiction we must look at the work "The Leaden Echo and the Golden Echo." This short story by Hopkins has two very important contradictions- beauty / ugliness and life / death. One of these, life and death, is depicted in the movie through dreams, art and war. The art of battle is depicted in the first major scene of the movie showing the slower, weaker, outnumbered barbarians getting defeated by the rich, powerful, quicker, smarter Roman army. Life and death is shown here as a battle where thousands of people lose their lives in the field. In other cases, we see life and death depicted in different ways in the movie. We see suicide, betrayal, revenge, innocence and destruction all as forms of death in this movie. Catholics dying as a result of playing games in the Coliseum could be considered innocent lives being lost because of one's religious belief. In this case the Roman rulers looked at it as a game as the Catholics competed in various death games, where the only way you could win is if you kill the other individual. It was a test of strength, endurance and skill, as Catholics and slaves were put up against arched enemies played by other Romans.

    We also see in this movie, death by betrayal. This is shown in the next major scenes-Commodus killing his father to become heir to the throne before his father bestowed the land to Maximus. This was a sort of betrayal to Commodus and he felt his father did not love him. So, he killed his father based on jealousy and ignorance and then tried to cover it up. I believe this scene in the movie is the most Keatsian because as Commodus is suffocating his father with his cloak, the camera focuses on a sculpture of his father's face just above the incident. In my opinion, the art depicts a person who is dying, but will live on in this sculpture of him. Later on in the movie, we see another sculpture of the fallen leader in front of the Coliseum before the battles begin. This again, shows that people through art, will never forget their fallen leader.

    Herman Melville, one of the late romantic writers, during the time of Keats and Hopkins, was also depicted in this movie through his use of separation of classes and sexes. Melville, in the short story, The

Paradise of Bachelors & the Tartars of Maids, had a much different outlook than Keats, when it came to separation of the class and of the sexes. In this story, Melville separates the sexes in groups, which had different jobs to do in the world. The men were the warriors or the hunters and women were nurturing and motherly, according to Melville. The men were depicted as bachelors of war and unrest and the women were depicted as nurturing maids who kept watch over the children. Melville also separated the class into rich and poor. The biggest of the classes was the middle class. In the movie, the poor could be depicted as the barbarians during the war scene and the slaves in combat. It shows you how a once-prominent general of the Roman army becomes a slave and how that slave survives to fight in the Coliseum till he meets his doom, as a result of trickery and deceit. The Barbarians were groups of people trying to save their land from being taken over by the Roman Empire. We can see the difference between rich and poor, by looking at the armor and weapons of both groups. The Roman Empire had more men, more advanced weapons and strong steel type armor as opposed to the barbarians who had very little armor, primitive type weapons and fewer men. Melville also tries to separate the sexes, unlike Keats who portrays them as together in life. This Melville depiction can also be seen in many instances throughout the film. In the movie we can see separation between brother and sister, father and son, church and state, the Senate and Ruler, women and men, Catholics and Romans and slave and ruler. We can see, in each instance destruction occurs, someone who dies or a hero that emerges. A good example of Melville, in the movie is the part where Marcus Areulius, the current ruler, wants to hand over the throne to someone other than his son, who is too incompetent to be a ruler. Commodus separates himself from his father when he apparently kills him in a fit of jealous rage. The daughter of Marcus Auerlius is inflamed by this and never trusted Commodus again throughout the whole movie. It came to a point where Commodus almost kills his sister and his sister's son because of an apparent attempt to free Maximus from capture.

Other examples of separation in the film can be seen after Commodus takes over the throne. He wants to separate the governmental entities. He wants to get rid of the Senate, so he can rule Rome by himself. This becomes a point of struggle in Rome and leads to a death of a Senator. Commodus believed in killing innocent Catholics for show in the Coliseum and he set a series of games to do just that. Here, we can see the separation of slave / Roman and church / state. The church did not believe in these acts of violence and totally downplayed what Commodus was doing. The state, in this case, was more powerful and continued through the games, making this a more tyrannical ruler. The Senate could not even stop him; it came to a point in the film, where the army wanted to free itself from such tyrannical rule. That was all stopped when Maximus' plan to escape was stopped.

Throughout the whole film, we are reminded of Keats and the theory of life is in art. Statues, structures, sculptures and dreams can be looked at as a depiction. Statues of Marcus Auerlius, the once famed ruler stood in front of the Coliseum. Statues of past rulers of the Roman Empire stood in the walls of the Coliseum. Most important, the art direction of the film brought back to life the once famed structure in the center of Rome, the Coliseum. Using computers, the art directors put together the building piece by piece. This alone is a Keatsian model of a structure that was once the center of activity and is now a memorial or relic of those who lost their lives in the center of the stadium. It was the first of its kind; a stadium built for games. It still stands in the center of Rome today; weathered and battered from natural disasters. Statues inside and around the outside of the ruler's palace, remembers those who graced its walls.

    The music score of this film also played a big role in this movie's success. The music followed the storyline very well and became more intense especially during the war and battle scene. You can say that the orchestra music throughout the movie could be related to Schubert and the way he portrayed things in life. Even though there were no words to the music in the movie, the music had a feeling of its own. The music expressed the different feelings of emotion Schubert tried to portray in his music. Emotions went from calm to fast and furious, so the music had to try to keep up. During the war scene the music started out as slow and promising for agreement; when the barbarians attacked, the music grew more intense because the war was about to start. You could feel the death and sorrow in the music at the end of the war scene. You could also feel the sorrow and mourning when Marcus Auerlius was pronounced dead. You could feel the jealousy and betrayal in the scenes to follow. You could also feel the anger and upheaval during the Coliseum and Rome scenes. Schubert was always one to express an emotion in his works. He mostly spoke about death and dying through song. This is why I compare the music in the movie to Schubert's music.

In conclusion, we can see that this film had all the parts, the people and the knowledge for being voted as best picture of the year 2000. We can also see how some of the writers and composers of the late romantic era may have had an effect on this film.

Table 3
Pictures of the Roman Republic
The Arch of Marcus Aurelius

The Arch of Marcus Aurelius from above

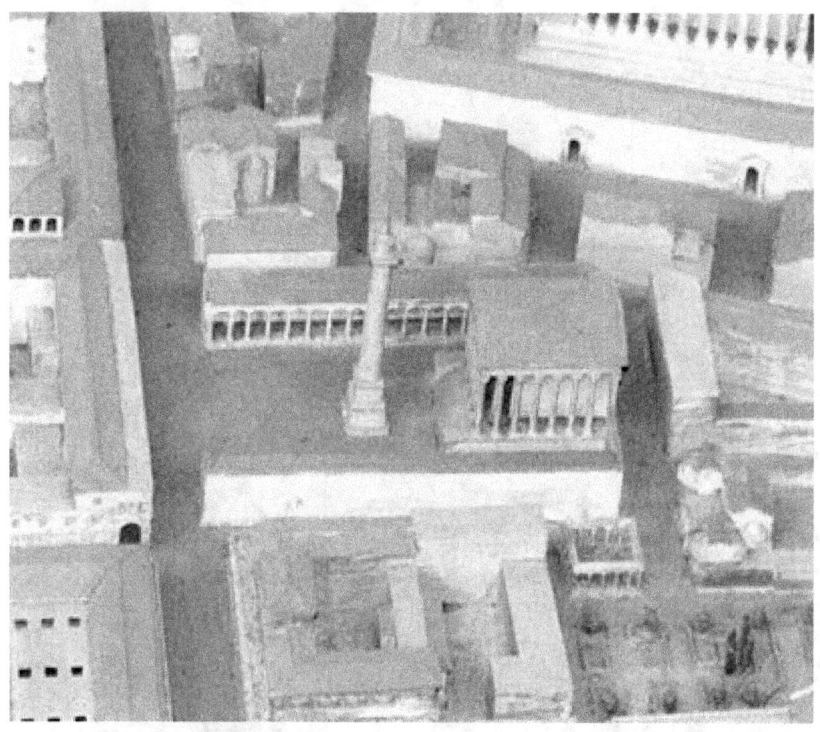

The Aqua Julia, one of the aqueducts on which the city's water supply depended. Built by Agrippa in 33 BC it brought water from the Alban Hills south east of Rome and was part of a major enlargement and modernization of water services under Augustus.

The Arch of Constantine

Castrensian Amphitheatre

Picture of the Amphitheatre from above

Aurelian began his new walls to defend Rome in AD 271 and they were completed under Probus in AD 280. They ranged more than twelve miles around Rome, were 60 feet high, were built of brick-faced concrete and had massive towers at intervals of about fifteen yards. The wall's height was later doubled by emperor Maxentius (AD 306-312). Much of the wall still exists today.

Above is a section near the Porta San Paolo (Porta Ostiensis), below a section, viewed from inside the city, close to the Castrensian Amphitheatre.

The Forum of Emperor Augustus

The forum restored to its original dimensions

The Imperial Palace

The Imperial Palace restored in all its beauty and grandeur in this model

The House of Vestals

The Pantheon

The Inside of the Pantheon in Rome

The Inside of the Pantheon in Rome (Part II)

Model of the Pantheon

American Socio-Economic Policy
Parts 5 and 6

We could get no further into the Æneid than
Matque altae moenia Romae,
—and the wall of high Rome,
before we were constrained to reflect by what myriad tests a work of genius has to be tried; that Virgil, away in Rome, two thousand years off, should have to unfold his meaning, the inspiration of Italian vales, to the pilgrim on New England hills. This life so raw and modern, that so civil and ancient; and yet we read Virgil mainly to be reminded of the identity of human nature in all ages, and, by the poet's own account, we are both the children of a late age, and live equally under the reign of Jupiter.

Henry David Thoreau (1817–1862), U.S. philosopher, author, naturalist
"A Walk to Wachusett" (1843)
The Writings of Henry David Thoreau, vol. 5, p. 138, Houghton Mifflin (1906)

Part 5
Overview of the American Socio-Economic System

The socio-economic system of America differs from the socio-economic system of the Roman Empire in few ways. America is built on freedom, democracy, freedom of expression, pursuit of happiness, liberty, diplomatic relations and international relations. America is built on the ideology of capitalism, which means free market. In the capitalistic society we see mergers, enterprises being built, stocks going public and U.S. savings bonds. There are also major institutions that are noted to be very powerful in the way of the social behavior of Americans. These institutions of social structure start out at the beginning of life and continue through death for most human beings. The economic structure and social structure of America does not flourish because of entertainment, but it primarily stays strong because of the work ethic and the amount of income brought in by major firms and businesses. On the other hand, Romans did not have the idea of the automobile and airplane, two methods of transportation that bring in billions of dollars a year. Transportation was one of the huge differences between Rome and America. Rome did not have the proper tools for building and getting around the city. The Romans used animals as a way of transportation around the city. Boats were a form of transportation used to increase the amount of trade between area of the world and it allowed for Rome's economy to expand as well.

However, other than boats and animals, everything was done by hand and foot. Therefore, we can see why there were massive deaths emerging as a result of Rome's lack of technology and construction. Construction in Rome was not like today in America. Today, the automobile, train, airplane, ships, etc. are all money and income makers for the United States. The economy of America is flourishing, because of these inventions, but do we use our money efficiently for importing and exporting purposes?

The social class structure was the same in both Rome and America, with one major difference. The people of Rome did not call their working class their middle class. There wasn't a middle class in Rome; it was just the rich and the poor. In America, because of the majority of working class Americans we see a huge middle class. Of course the question still arises, is the United States government corrupt and how does it use the people's tax money? According to writer Richard Vedder of USA Today, "The U.S. can be said to have a dual economy…there is the private-sector economy, which produces goods and services in response to the wants of consumers and businesses… there is the government sector, which largely redistributes the income."[167] According to this quote from Vedder, the government redistributes people's tax money after it is received. The money goes into so-called governmental projects to better the society. Does it really happen that way? In my opinion, probably not because the government is so selfish and self-righteous that they do not put the money into certain major project like education, crime, the environment, etc. In my opinion, government allocates money into public work projects that are not that important to the American people.

Social institutions such as the family, schools and churches teach the youth of the country how to grow up and live a good, healthy, prosperous life. The family in America was considered a very important institution in the 20th century. According to Kathy Slobogin, of CNN news:

"The survey found that women feel more overworked than men. Now, it's interesting because it doesn't seem to have anything to do with whether or not the women have children. When they analyze the data, they found that the major difference between women and men was that women reported more multi-tasking on the job, and more interruptions in their workday, and that these were the things that were associated with overwork."[168]

With the introduction of women into the workforce today, it is nearly impossible for a family to hold together. According to the American Academy of Pediatrics, "Family relationships may suffer if both parents want to work but only one has a job. Problems also can occur if there is competition or resentment because one parent is earning more money than the other. Such conflicts can strain the marriage, and may make the children feel threatened and insecure. With both parents working, the need for mutual support and communication is even more important."[169] This is why today we see so many of single parent families. As a woman's monetary income is needed to support the household, therefore, stress is at an all-time high in America. Divorces are on the rise and men and women feel they could provide for themselves. Women feel they can provide for themselves now, therefore, they do not need a man to play that role. According to the American Academy of the Child, "While parents may be devastated or relieved by the divorce, children are invariably frightened and confused by the threat to their security. Some parents feel so hurt or overwhelmed by the divorce that they may turn to the child for comfort or direction. Divorce can be misinterpreted by children unless parents tell them what is happening, how they are involved and not involved and what will happen to them."[170] The divorce rate is high. As result, the family breaks apart and the children are stuck in the middle. Most children do not understand divorce until they grow older. According to the majority, that men and women should be on the same page to have a good strong 50/50 relationship in today's world. However since family values are a thing of the past, men and women feel better living on their own. According to the American Academy of Pediatrics,

> "Parents need to clearly understand that homosexual orientation is not a mental disorder. The cause(s) of homosexuality are not fully understood. However, a person's sexual orientation is not a matter of choice. In other words, individuals have no more choice about being homosexual than heterosexual. All teenagers do have a choice about their

expression of sexual behaviors and lifestyle, regardless of their sexual orientation."[171]

In today's ever changing society, there is also the introduction of the gay and lesbian families. According to the American Academy of Pediatrics, "It is important for parents to understand their teen's homosexual orientation and to provide emotional support. Parents often have difficulty accepting their teen's homosexuality for some of the same reasons that the youngster wants to keep it secret. Gay or lesbian adolescents should be allowed to decide when and to whom to disclose their homosexuality. Parents and other family members may gain understanding and support from organizations such as Parents, Families and Friends of Lesbians and Gays (PFLAG)."[172] Many in America misunderstand the premise of homosexual marriage. Will it affect the population of America? Will this lead to a lower birth rate and higher death rates? Will gay and lesbian families teach their children to be homosexual? These are just some of the questions that America is pondering about this issue. One of the other main questions is: What is the definition of a homosexual in society? According to the American Academy of Pediatrics, "Homosexuality is the persistent sexual and emotional attraction to someone of the same sex. It is part of the range of sexual expression. Many gay and lesbian individuals first become aware of and experience their homosexual thoughts and feelings during childhood and adolescence. Homosexuality has existed throughout history and across cultures."[173]

As for the education in schools money is a factor. Teachers do not receive an adequate salary in today's society, therefore, we are lacking in the education system. Education is important for a young growing child. It is important for children to learn about the world around them. This is how society grows. In my opinion, most of the income from taxes should go into the education of the children of this country. They are the future and if they are not taught effectively, the future of this great power may be in jeopardy.

During the time of the Great Depression in the 1930s, people were economically and socially in trouble. The U.S. dollar was worth not even a penny after the stock market crash of 1929. The people were in a confused and bewildered state, looking for help in any way from their government. Franklin Delano Roosevelt, the only president to get elected to four consecutive terms, helped the people through this with the creation of jobs through the creation of federal and state public works projects and through the formation of agency within the government such as the Tennessee Valley Authority and the creation of Social Security Benefits. The creation of jobs spurred the market and got its final push from WWII. We were out of the depression in the 1940's and prospered until the 1960's. The 1960's became a problematic period in the United States.

With the emergence of the followers of the Counter- Cultural Revolution, the social structure of the United States declined, bringing the economic structure down with it. During the 1970's there were points of stagflation under President Richard Nixon and President Gerald Ford. There was also a period of high energy and oil prices under President Jimmy Carter. This Counter-Cultural Revolution began in the 1960's and lasted until the 1980s. People, during this period of time, did not trust their government due to what they felt were bad decisions, including the Vietnam War. People protested for peace. The minds of the population were changed to more liberal kinds of thinking such as freedom of expression, freedom of orientation and freedom of speech. Drugs, sex and alcohol were good ways to describe the theme of America during this revolution. "Rock-n-Roll," was the music of the time and tended to let out the anger of the people within the music. This could have been a time of revolt against the government, but the United States put in place strict laws. These laws restricted people from revolting against the government. This could have led to massive social civil war in the 1960s, but the people were more reserved because of these strict laws. Social confusion could lead to civil war and the end of an empire, but in this case it was just a factor in the decline of a great power.

      How does this all compare to Rome? Firstly, Rome was not governed in states or provinces. Ancient Rome was governed as a whole. The capital of the Roman Empire was Rome and only Rome; there were no outside governing bodies such as mayors and governors running the empire. The ruler or emperor was the sole leader of the Roman Empire. There was one social structure and one economic structure, whereas the United States had the same but within each state there was a social and economic structure. This allows for differentiation from state to state. Living conditions are varied by state. In Rome there was one common living structure. The laws/rules and regulations are different in each state. In Rome there was one common set of laws. United States land was acquired, whereas Rome's land was conquered and taken over. United States' government was more democratic, whereas Rome was more tyrannical, but both governments were corrupt especially when it comes to the tax income. Basically, both Rome and America had the same structures with different features. Both had the social minorities, both had the family and both had these very important institutions. Economy was based on different things. American economy is based on the stock market and capitalism, whereas Rome's focus was more of the barter / trade. So the conclusion that we can reach here is that both Rome and the United States are similar in structures but are different in policy-making and governmental structuring.

Part 6
Darwin's political and scientific effects on literature and society in America and Europe during the late 1800's and early 1900's

7.1: The Introduction

One of the most influential authors and theorists of America and modern day is Charles Darwin. This man single-handedly changed the minds of societies and present day authors through his theories of life, science and nature. Darwin can be looked at as the Marcus Aurelius of our time. Darwin was a philosopher and a leader in his own right. He taught the world about scientific structure in society and he also gave us such theories as "survival of the fittest" and "natural selection." He can be looked at as a modern philosopher with the power to change and manipulate society's minds. Marcus Aurelius was the source of political and societal thought in Ancient Rome. Darwin can be said to be like Marcus Aurelian, because he had a certain effect not only on society, but on literature and the arts as well. Darwin was big on science and scientific methods. This part will be about how Darwin's theories affected literature and society in the 19th and 20th centuries in England, during the Victorian Era of writing and in the United States during the time of "The Scopes Trial."

Darwinian Theory began in the early to mid-1800's affecting both the ideas of societal evolution and literary evolution. Societal meaning "real life" or reality rather than fictional, affecting the people of one's culture and beliefs of a particular environment. Literary meaning "fantasy life" or fictional rather than reality, affecting one's mind and memory when reading a literary work written during the Victorian Era. The Victorian Era was a time of both societal change and a change in literary writing. This enlightenment led to a change in people's thought process, which led to people not following the norms of society and changing their traditions and customs. These changes led to wars, strikes, protests, movements and upheavals in the coming years especially in Great Britain, western Europe, as well as, parts of eastern Europe and in the United States. In some cases these changes led to civil war within one's own country. To better understand Darwinian theory, there are concepts one must understand to seek out examples of history and literary writing. Darwinian Theory is based on a series of important concepts, one of the most important being the concept of "survival of the fittest." Other important concepts to understand when thinking about Darwinian Theory are "The Descent of Man," "Theory of Domestication," "Natural Selection," "Sexual Selection," and "The Theory of Adaptation." All of these ideas and theories of Darwin can be explained both in a literary and a societal matter. Both literary thinking and societal thinking can also be compared and contrasted by looking at these theories as well.

7.2: The Early Years and Life of Darwin

To better understand Darwin you must look back at his early years. Charles Darwin was born on February 12, 1809 into a well-to-do family. Charles was comfortable and secure within the Darwin and Wedgwood families because they were rich. His mother was part of the Wedgwood family, and Charles himself later in life would marry into the Wedgwood family by marrying his cousin Emma. He was the son and grandson of prosperous physicians. When Charles tried to get into the medical field he found it to be dull and boring. So he followed the advice of his father and went to Cambridge to study to become a minister.[174] He of course would later study scientific theories, which were disputed by most religious people, including one, William Paley, who would criticize Darwin in his book "Natural Theology," and come up with his own idea or theory called "Intelligent Design." Intelligent Design was a more religious idea or more God-like theory that William Paley explored. An example of Intelligent Design would be "The Designs Implies a Designer," or "The Watch Implies the Watchmaker." Basically, it means for everything that is created, a creator is needed and being a religious figure, Paley tries to imply that God is the creator of the world through use of these examples. Other critics of Darwin came in the early and late 20th century with the belief that Darwin's theories were fanatical and outlandish. Some of these critics are Pope John Paul II, Eugene C. Scott and religious groups such as The Jewish Orthodox

Creationists and The Islamic Creationists. The Scopes Trial and other trials of the early 20th century made Darwinian Theories illegal in the education system. Students were not allowed to learn about these theories and it was basically ousted from the institution. Although it was ousted, we still saw Darwinian theory play itself out in the 20th century from mostly a societal prospective.

Darwin was less interested in the field of theology at Cambridge but he was more interested in Entomology. Entomology, according to Appleman, was a popular Victorian hobby which Darwin took part in by collecting and studying beetles.[175] To obtain his degree from Cambridge, Charles took three years of courses dealing with the classics, mathematics and philosophy. At the same time, he was trying to obtain his degree. He studied not only insects, but also the natural sciences (biology, geology and taxonomy etc…) with professors like botanist John Stevens Henslow, Geologist Adam Sedgwick and well-known philosopher of science, William Whewell.[176] In 1831, Charles Darwin received his B.A. degree from Cambridge.

Darwin learned plenty of information from his grandfather, Erasmus. According to Appleman, Erasmus came up with two very important theories being "The Notion of Mutability of Species," and "Embryonic Development." An example of this is the metamorphosis of a caterpillar into a moth. Erasmus believed in changes by domestication and habitation, which inturn affects the life span of a given animal or mammal. Erasmus Darwin could not explain the theory of adaptation and adapting to one's environment. This would later be explored and theorized by his grandson Charles Darwin. On December 27, 1831, at the age of 22, Darwin left England for a five-year journey around the globe.[177] After this five-year journey, Darwin became intellectually and deliberately domestic because of a mysterious, chronic illness. He suffered with heart palpitations and daily debilitating nausea. His wife Emma took care of her husband and their ten children and she sustained him in his work, asking him challenging questions, writing countless letters at his dictation and helping correct the proofs of his books he was writing.[178] Despite his illness Darwin worked every day on his so-called contributions to science. He wrote many literary works from 1845-1881. The most famous of his writing were: The Voyage of the Beagle (1845), The Origin of Species (1859), The Descent of Man (1871), The Expression of the Emotions in Man and Animals (1872), The Formation of Vegetable Mould Through the Action of Earthworms (1881). He also wrote an autobiography of himself and other correspondences on scientific matters.[179] Darwin later died at the age of 73 in the year of 1882 and was buried at Westminster Abbey, which was a rare and national honor. He was buried a few feet from famed British scientist, Issac Newton.[180] Now that we have a better understanding of Charles Darwin's life, we can better understand his theories and ideas and show examples from history and literary works that prove his theories. Then, we can see effects of Darwinism on society and see the changing effects of Darwinism in the Victorian era. Evolution is one of the larger points raised by Darwin in most of his writings. To better understand his theory of evolution, we must look at specific books and events of history.

7.3: The Descent of Man

To better understand the writing styles and metaphors of Darwin we can look at his book *The Descent of Man* in detail. In this book, we can see Darwin's use of metaphors and examples to explain his theories. Darwin's writing style varied throughout *The Descent of Man* and his other theories. Darwin liked to tell a story and give many examples to back up his point on specific issues regarding animals and humans. Darwin was also said to refer many literary texts to also prove a point. He was mainly a man of imagination; who believed science was the language of literature and was very subjective and narrative in his writing. At some points in *The Descent of Man,* you can say that Darwin was writing a journal of day's events. He was also very aggressive in his theories. He always tried to make his point on particular issues stand out from the others. Being a man of imagination, Darwin used his mind to develop theories that could explain most of civilization. One such theory was the theory of evolution and adaptation based on the scale of natural selection.[181] Darwin says, "Adaptations may be structural, physiological or behavioral." He also goes on to say," They may be genetically simple or complex. They may involve individual cells or subcellular components, or whole organs or organ systems. They may be highly specific…. or they may be general."[182] This quote from the Appleman book, describes the many ways adaptation can occur in the mind of Darwin. The Descent of Man was a theory based hugely on sexual selection and how females choose their mates both in the animal kingdom and amongst the human population. You can say that once you finish reading Darwin, his theories are more argumentative toward all others. He always tries to involve some type of conflict or even write in a tragic or comic style. He likes to stick to his beliefs but sites others and uses other's writings for examples. One of the major issues seen in *The Descent of Man* is mammals vs. humans and the similarities and differences between the two. Mammals do not match up with humans based on brain capacity usage, but they are similar when talking about reproductive development, the muscular structure, bone and skeletal structure and the use of the five senses. Darwin describes one of these differences as follows:" The structure of the hand in this respect may be compared with that of vocal cords, which in apes are used for uttering various signal cries, as in one genus, musical cadences…."[183] He also goes on to say," Their hands do not serve for locomotion so well as the feet of a dog; as may be seen in such monkeys as the chimpanzee and orange, which walk on the outer margins of the palms, or on the knuckles. Their hands however are admirably adapted for climbing trees."[184] He also states," Other monkeys open mussel-shells with the two thumbs."[185] He tries to state these points as examples for explaining his theory of the descent of man. Moreover, he tries to explain his theory of natural selection with the use of these and other examples, such as: "Man in the rudest state in which he now exists is the most dominant animal that has ever appeared on this earth."[186] This statement by Darwin can also be said to explain another one of his theories, "Survival of the Fittest." He also goes on to say, "He has invented and is able to use various weapons, tools, traps…with which he defends himself, kills or catches prey and otherwise obtains foods."[187] This quote basically states the differences of natural selections and the differences of the descent of man. Men are more powerful according to Darwin but there are some similarities. He also states that humans were created with more advanced brains. Apes were the examples used to show more primitive creatures and how they measure up to humans. Darwin believes that humans are very advanced, especially when you look at organ systems and body structure. Darwin states that, "These several inventions, by results of the development of his powers of observation, memory, curiosity, imagination and reason."[188] He then goes on to state refuting comments made by Mr. Wallace by saying, "I cannot, therefore, understand how it is that Mr. Wallace maintains, that natural selection could only have endowed the savage with a brain a little superior to that of an ape."[189] This quote explains the power of the human brain as superior to all others including those of apes.

The Descent of Man was written by Darwin to explain various scientific theories of nature. One of those theories that are discussed could be relevant to both societal and literary evolution. The first theory is "Survival of the Fittest." This theory can be found in both societal and literary evolution. Literary works, including Middlemarch and Aurora Leigh embody the ideas of "Survival of the Fittest," through the evolution of the environment and evolution of the characters both physically and mentally. For example in the novel Middlemarch, there is an underlying theme of oppression and discrimination. Discrimination against age, sex and familial status were all recognized in this novel. This discrimination occurred because of changes in the literary environment and changes in society. Men oppressed women for centuries, but in this novel we see a different side to women. We see the strength and courage of women. We see women expressing opinions and different lifestyles. At the same time the book was written there was a major change in society, affecting almost the whole world. This change was called the "Enlightenment Era." People started thinking for themselves and having their own opinions, especially those groups oppressed in the past. "Survival of the Fittest," can be seen as a good example here. Even in today's American society the oppressed people, who are the minorities survived to speak their mind. The formerly oppressed people are now rising up to become stronger than the oppressors (The White Caucasian Men). It was even seen in the Roman Empire with the idea of the gladiator and oppression of minority groups, including the Christians. Although, many people were oppressed during the time of the Romans, the oppressed survived in the end to see the rise of Christianity and the fall of the Roman Republic. As for the literary oppression we can see women getting stronger in the novel, "Middlemarch." "Survival of the Fittest," is well- explained more in depth in the next sub-section of this part.

7.4: Literary evolution of the Victorian Era and Charles Darwin's theories

To better understand Darwin in a more literary sense, we must look at some literary works of the Victorian Era and see how the authors express theories of evolution in their works. In literary examples, we will find that the more natural aspects of biology are not explained. The theories will be explained with themes, settings, character evolvement, character personalities, and social problems of the time. Psychology of the author and of the characters is another major aspect used in literary works to explain the theories of Darwin through the mind of the author. To explain his theories in a more societal sense, we can use historical events and happenings. We can also examine changes in society within minority groups within countries, especially those outside the United States. Societal is more historical and factual. Literary is more psychological and exploratory.

7.4.a: Middlemarch by George Eliot and Today's Society Co-mingle

  The first of the literary works that will be explored for evolutionary purposes will be the novel of Middlemarch by George Eliot. George Eliot had a very religious family but she refused to attend church and she had many family problems early in her life. She finished writing the book Middlemarch in the year 1876, but the setting of the story was in 1832 and 1833, the height of Great Britain's prominence. She lived from 1819 to 1880. She lost religious faith as she grew up due to rationalists. George Eliot then married George Henry Louise, who was married previously and could not get a divorce from his cheating wife after 24 years of marriage. Eliot was a very insecure person and needed a man to support her. She was accepted in the Victorian Era as a woman of strong moral. Little did people know, that she, and other authors of the time would change societal thinking forever, especially for women. As we can see from this brief biography of George Eliot, she is a very insecure woman with strong moral stature. She had marital problems and family problems and she lost her religious faith as a child. Therefore, we can see why she would write a story about three relationships during the time Great Britain was at its prominence. We can also see why feminism was a major theme of *Middlemarch* because Eliot had a mind of her own and we will see the evolution of the writer in the characters throughout the novel. We can also see how her marital problems in real life played out in the novel through such characters as Dorothea and Mary Garth. We can also see the female dominance in the novel as more fictional than societal, because in reality, women were still fighting for rights, still fighting for their education and still fighting for their independence in Great Britain during the Victorian Era. Eliot, through the novel, expresses the need for women to stand up for what they believe and have a mind of their own.

After reading the whole novel of Middlemarch, we can see that Eliot gives an author's twist to evolution in many aspects of life and figurative imagination. Eliot was good at telling a story within a story. She also kept the reader interested with the many themes that she tried to express in this story; evolution and constant change was one of them. We can see the constant progression of each character's lifestyles throughout the story. Evolution means constant change within an individual or object evolution is seen through the eyes of three strong women in their quest to follow and reach their dreams. To fulfill their dreams was a must, and Eliot made that a constant theme in this book.

Evolution being the constant theme of this book can be seen throughout its setting of the book, as well as, the three main relationships between Dorothea and Mr. Casaubon, Lydgate and Rosamond and Fred and Mary Garth. Evolution can also be seen through each character's dreams and personalities. As the characters adjusted throughout the novel due to the changing times, their personalities changed with them. Eliot portrayed her characters in a life-like way making them stand out to the audience reading the book.

At the time this book was being written, evolution was taking place all over the world especially in England where the story was set. England during this time (1830's -1880's) was considered to be the superpower of the world because the United States was still an up and coming entity and was not yet industrialized. England was a constantly changing nation during the 1830's. This could be looked at as a type of enlightenment of the modern world. It can be seen throughout the novel as a type of evolution of the environment. The novel of Middlemarch was written in the 1870s, but the story itself was set in 1832, which was a very good time in Great Britain. During this time, the Great Reform Bill was adopted and major political changes were taking place in the British Empire. Political power was in the hands of the Tories for years. During this period of time Britain was undergoing change in the political system. The Tories gave up the political power and the political majority changed over. Only males had the right to vote for their elected officials. They finally had a say in who would represent them in politics. This was a period of change not only in politics, but also people changed their outlooks on life and within their relationships changed as well. There was also a stronger sense of community that was never felt before all across Britain and most importantly the whole of Europe felt this change as well. The evolution of Europe and Great Britain is expressed through the setting chosen by Eliot. Eliot chose this period of time to put in the book to show evolution and change in the environment. The themes of this novel are constantly in evolution or change; therefore, we can see a type of figurative evolution as well throughout the entire novel.

Other methods of evolution used in this novel, by George Eliot were variation, diversification and the metaphor of the web, which could be considered a notion. Metaphor of the web, meaning intermingling or various ideas that tie into one big idea just like a web joined in the middle. Variation is the key to evolutionary development and used the most by Eliot in this novel. Diversification can be seen in the different personalities of the characters. Each character is very diverse and reacts differently to the same problems. Polarity is another method of evolution used in this novel. This structural principle is used to show opposites within the novel. Some examples of this would be youth and age, life and death, attach vs. need, tradition vs. new, great expectations and the loss of great expectations, and country and town. In looking at polarity between characters, we can see that the best couple would have been Lydgate and Dorothea, but they never get together in the novel. In looking at the three relationships portrayed by Eliot in this novel we can see different problems in each of the relationships, different personalities and different attitudes toward changes in the environment.

The meaning of enlightenment, according to the Webster Dictionary, was "a specific period in European history when reason and change in society took place developing a keen sense of thought amongst people of a certain group or culture." Eliot beautifully portrays this through the three women characters, which dominate the men in this story. Eliot, to show the evolution of a woman's thought process, gave all three women in the novel the power of choice and a strong personality that which the men in the story backed away from. Feminist overtones can be seen in this book and that, in itself, is evolutionary material. Feminism is evolutionary because women before this time in history could not have a mind of their own. The Victorian Era brought about an evolutionary process in the way women thought and the way women acted. This idea quickly spread throughout Europe and Americas. You can see this by looking at the first two chapters of *Middlemarch*. An example can be seen in with Dorothea and Celia. They were sisters who were born with different personalities. We can also see an evolution of the sisters from the beginning to the end of the book. Dress played a huge role in the times; the better dressed you were the higher the rank. Dorothea was the more outspoken of the two sisters. She was also distinguished, intelligent and filled with common sense. She was also a very religious figure. Celia, on the other hand, was the quieter of the two sisters. She was always looked upon as second, behind Dorothea. Men of the time tended to like Celia better because she wasn't a believer in women being strong and outspoken. She accepted her place in society, unlike her sister who was a rebel. Men feared Dorothea because of her temperament and beliefs. She believed, and this is where you can see the psychology come out, that women deserved a better place in society. With certain things she did-for example, horseback riding-men were scared that they were being outdone. It was unheard of for a woman to do certain things in society and Dorothea, because of her psychology, wanted to prove them wrong. The psychology of women plays a big role in the methodology of feminism, especially in today's society. Dorothea evolved from a woman of focus and understanding into a woman who was more laid-back and took anything that came her way. Celia looked like the more aggressive sister by the end of the story and this all has to do with the evolution of a character's lifestyle due to an outside environmental change or previous relationships or societal change. We can also see feminism evolving with the story as well and the determining factor was the society that these women were living in. Feminism flourished in this novel because Eliot wanted to show that the women of the book were more powerful than the men and therefore, the feminist overtones in the novel were dominant. The setting was one of feminism. We can see that through the eyes of the characters Dorothea, Rosamond and Mary Garth. Most importantly Dorothea and Celia are focused in on as the women of change and as the women who will move forward the feminist ideal in *Middlemarch*.

    We can see throughout books 3, 4 and 5 a strong sense of the feminine ideal and the beliefs that strive in the female ideology. Being that the Victorian Era was a changing time, Dorothea wanted to prove her strength and will to her male counterparts. Three prominent male figures throughout the story were Mr. Casaubon, whom Dorothea fell for because of his sense of humor and his intelligence, Sir James Chettam and Mr. Brooke, the sister's uncle who had a strong sense of masculinity and refused to hear anything about the feminine ideal and of a woman having her own mind. All these minds clash in various chapters of this book due to the evolution of the times. Celia and Dorothea have two famous arguments in the book. The arguments were about the mother's jewelry and about Mr. Casaubon and Sir James Chettam (which one should Dorothea should pick). Celia believed that Sir James and Dorothea were great together. Eliot states about the personalities of Dorothea and Celia," She was usually spoken of as being remarkably clever, but with the addition that her sister Celia had more common sense."[190] Eliot states about the religious beliefs of Dorothea," Dorothea knew many passages of Pascal's Pensees and of Jeremy Taylor by heart; and to her the destinies of mankind, seen by the light Christianity, made the solitudes of feminine fashion appear an occupation for Bedlam."[191] She also goes on to says about Dorothea," Her mind was theoretic, and yearned by its nature after some lofty conception of the world, which might frankly include the parish of Tipton and her own rule of conduct there...."[192] These statements made a strong example for Dorothea's feminine fashion, religious beliefs and theoretic mind. Dorothea, being the feminine idealist wanted a man with intelligence, wanted a man who can make a strong opinion without the help of the female and a man who she knew would protect her. To Dorothea, to have power over men was important and she saw that in Mr. Casaubon, whom she saw as a weak old man. Celia saw Mr. Casaubon as ugly and shallow. Dorothea told Celia to stop looking at looks ("animals") and look at the personality; Dorothea saw a great man in Mr. Casaubon. Eliot states about the feminine ideal the following, "Nothing could hinder it but her love of extremes, and her insistence on regulating life according to notions which might cause a wary man to hesitate before he made her an offer, or even might lead her at last to refuse all offers."[193] This statement best describes the personality of Dorothea toward her male counterparts and a strong sense of the feminine ideal. The Feminine ideal had a major effect throughout Dorothea's life. Even today, we can see women who express the feminine ideal. Women in today's society are equal to men in more ways than one. It's the feminine ideal that pushes women to get more and this is one of the evolutionary processes brought forth by Eliot in the novel.

This book contrasts many different personality traits. It shows us or teaches us how relationships can stay together or breaks apart based on people's perceptions and beliefs in one another. The evolution of personality traits in this novel is very overpowering. We can see characters that were once objects to follow, fall to certain environment or societal changes. Personalities changed from happiness to sadness or dismay. We can see a number of changes taking place within the three major relationships of the story. Understanding, trust, honesty and respect are traits that would change from book 1 through the final book of the novel. There are many examples that could explain this evolution. For example, Dorothea and Mr. Casaubon had a variety of problems. One problem was the age factor and another problem was the insecurity. Both of these characters used each other as a crutch to get past their insecurities. Another example would be the relationship between Fred and Mary Garth (the so-called opposites attract relationship). This relationship was a little more stable than the others, but yet again these two characters use each other's personality traits to move along in life. Fred is lazy and Mary Garth is insecure with herself. Mary Garth proved to be the strongest of all the females in this book because she was built with a strong personality and also built with a lot less insecurity as the other two women. In the case of Lydgate and Rosamond, Rosamond is strong, nimble and smart, but Lydgate is an egomaniac who thinks about himself and his ideas. Society plays a big role in the way Lydgate thinks. Rosamond has a developing insecurity problem throughout the whole novel. Lydgate will take advice of others and care for others to a point, but when it comes to himself he wants to get ahead before everyone else. In my opinion, Lydgate is a doctor and doctors have trouble creating relations with others. These are all examples of the evolution of relationships through changes society and the environment. All three women characters have a developing insecurity throughout the novel leading to misunderstanding and doubt of their loved ones. Looks and status in society are the two major insecurities seen in this novel.

During the story we can see that Eliot gives sympathy to most of her characters. One character, due to the adaptation to the environment and her evolution throughout the novel, Mary Garth, did not need any sympathy because of her strong will to move forward.

Darwin's theories and many of today's societal issues can be seen in this novel. "Survival of the Fittest," is prevalent in within the book as Eliot looked at various relationship and various relations between friends. This theory can also be seen in the environment of the literary. As the environment so did the characters. Some of the characters adapted to the change well and other did not leading to confusion and bewilderment. Some American issues could be seen in this novel as well. One of the most important issues brought up in the novel was that of feminism and how feminism affected the evolution of society. Other issues that are prevalent in the novel include, oppression, discrimination, marital status, divorce and marriage, ageism, relationships between people and relationships between societies.

7.4.b: Aurora Leigh and shades of Darwinian Overtones in this Novel

After better understanding George Eliot's writing, we can compare George Eliot with other literary greats of the Victorian Era and see what is different or the same about most Victorian writers. Evolution of the writing style can also be seen with use of poetry, sonnets, current events and people's experiences. We can compare George Eliot with Elizabeth Browning, another Victorian writer who wrote the novel Aurora Leigh. In this comparison we need to look at the evolution of writing style, themes, settings and plots. This poetry by Elizabeth Browning has many themes and symbols that describe both the characters and the setting. Many social issues were occurring during the time the poetry was written. Aurora Leigh the character was seen as a character with feminist overtones, which thought for herself and became independent after she found out that poetry was to be the occupation or her life. Browning expresses through the character her willingness to better herself in life and a willingness to be a positive role model for women during the time. One major issue or theme seems to be that of prostitution. This poetry was written to condemn such acts and portray women in a more positive light. It was one of the many social ills of the time. One of the outlaying themes of the poetry is how Browning wanted males to respect women more, not for their bodies but for their work ethic and brains. All Browning's poetry dealt with a particular social evil. She talked a lot about current events in her poetry and this fed through the characters. Another major theme is the emergence of nature in poetry and the freedom of expressing sexual acts in a poem. Evolution according to Browning, is different than evolution according to Eliot. Eliot's evolution is seen through her characters and environment changes; Browning, on the other hand, concentrates on the evolution of the education system and the institution of the school. Browning explored sexuality more than in prior reading such as *Middlemarch*, which had to do so more discreetly. Browning called her main character (Aurora Leigh), a "white knight." This description of the main character made Browning stand out, put a spotlight on her and was looked at as a hero (No woman during this time was looked at as a hero). In the novel of *Middlemarch*, Eliot makes the women characters powerful and strong, but doesn't portray a woman figure as a hero as Browning did in her novel. The major prevalent theme of the *Aurora Leigh* was the education of women in Britain later in the Victorian Era. Browning believed in the education of females just as Virginia Woolf (another Victorian Era writer) did in her novel *The Three Guineas*. Education and relationships were prevalent in all three novels but there was a different twist used by each author. All three books were set in Britain during the Victorian Era, during the height of Great Britain's prominence as a superpower in the late 19th century. The education factor is more prevalent in Aurora Leigh but can be seen in Woolf's novel as well. We can also see a vastly different writing style between the three books. At this point we can see the evolution of the writing styles. Woolf writes more from experience, Eliot uses more imagination and Browning uses poetry.

Aurora Leigh was very attached to her father in the story. Her father lived in Italy and was very highly educated. He wanted his daughter to get the best education and felt his daughter was very intelligent. Education consisted of a number of books in the father's library. Therefore she learned various topics such as writing proper English, learning different languages giving her a vast background in communication, geography, music, and science (such as biology, chemistry, astronomy and physics). She learned how to be independent and outspoken in her opinion and she learned to think for herself and come up with her own opinions on important issues. She also received a very liberal education being that she lived in a very liberal family. The discovery of poetry was most important in her life. It gave her self-confidence, freedom to express herself in any way she wished and gave her that sense of independence. She was successful in writing all different types of poetry. Aurora liked to write sonnets and, as she got older, she started writing more epic poetry. We can see how the story of Aurora Leigh embodied the ideas of education and the sense of evolution within it. The evolution of the educational system in developed nations did not really come about until the early 20th century. Browning through her poetry, wanted to see an evolution of education because women were illiterate and educated very little. This is a perfect example of women being held back by society. We can also see the evolution of writing style; poetry became a new way to express feelings and emotions.

7.4.c: The Three Guineas and Darwinian Overtones of "Survival of the Fittest"

Virginia Woolf's book, "The Three Guineas," is a vastly different style of writing. Virginia Woolf writes more from experience, being she lived in England during the Victorian Era. It's more based on the point of view of a woman. It was written in a more personal view rather than a factual one. Woolf's book is focused more on education, the teaching of history as propaganda, peace rather than war and the dissection of modern society. Woolf, being a woman, experienced how women were treated in developed nations such as the United States and Europe. They did not have an education, half the woman population was illiterate and women were treated like they were second-class citizens. She was part of Peace Organization that was looking for ways to stop war rather than continue it. According to Woolf, it is natural for men to fight, based on hierarchy and the man's notion of leadership in the military and in the government. Woolf saw all leaders as the same; Hitler, Mussolini, Churchill and FDR were categorized in the same manner. She considered them all regimes and viewed their leadership as one with differences between them. One of the major themes of this book was focused on the education of women and children. She believes that children were taught history not based on fact but more based on personal belief. History in school was based more on false beliefs than true fact. Women were not educated and Woolf wanted to rebuild the universities for women in England. According to a direct quote from Woolf," Our country treated us like slaves." She is basically is describing how women were treated in England and by other developed nations.[194] Woolf's book had a lot of feminist overtones in it, which basically described the feeling of most women in developed nations during the 1930's Great Depression era. Firstly, we can see, the evolution of the writing style, from fictional and poetry, to more of a feeling and emotion based on experience. The experience factor in Woolf's book is very important to the plot and themes of the story. This story can be looked at societal evolution as well because of the use of life experiences. Woolf portrays herself in the character, which is fictional but, being she lived through these oppressive times for women, she expresses her thoughts through the mind of the fictional character. The evolution of the educational system can be seen in this book as well. This book expresses the idea of people adapting to their environment and wanted to change the way society thinks.

7.5: Societal Evolution according to Darwin in America and Rome

After looking at the evolution of writing styles, characters, personalities of characters, themes, plots and settings we can get a better understanding of fictional or literary evolution in the world today. Societal evolution is a much different way of looking at evolution. Societal evolution deals with current events, cycles of events in history, changes in the natural environment, change in social structure and social status, changes in world tradition and philosophy, changes in customs and most importantly changes in people toward their environment.

The books used to prove the point about the constant evolution of society, were books written by Victorian Era, British writers. We can see that Darwin shows up in all three of these books. We can see the theories of "survival of fittest" and "natural selection" within books such as *Middlemarch* and *The Three Guineas*. Books like these have several characters which show evolution with the setting and plot of the book. Darwin, being a Marcus Aurelius type theorist and philosopher, is discussed not only in manuscripts, but in real life as well. Like life is constantly moving, the life of a book is constantly moving. Everything evolves and everything changes over time. It is up to us to examine the effect on the people and the society. How is society affected? How are the minds of people affected? How is literature affected?

What does Charles Darwin's ideas have to do with the Roman Empire? Well, if you look at the Roman Empire, you can see Darwin's ideas coming to light, especially "Survival of the Fittest." Darwin, who explained "survival of the fittest" within scientific terms, can be seen in the Roman political and societal structure. Examples of this would be gladiatorial combat, imperialism of outside lands weaker than the empire, the ruler vs. the people, and society vs. the ruler. "Natural selection" could also be seen in Ancient Rome. We can see this as the persecution of the minorities and of the Christians. Because they were different Roman society did not protect or accept these people. Appleman's book states about natural selection:

"It may be said that natural selection is daily and hourly scrutinizing, throughout the world, every variation, even the slightest; rejecting that which is bad, preserving and adding up which is good; silently and insensibly working whenever opportunity offers, at the improvement of each organic being in relation to its organic and inorganic conditions of life..."[195]

Appleman also states, "Charles Darwin devised the concept of natural selection while attempting to explain the evolution of organic diversity."[196] We can see from these two quotes that Darwin's theories can be seen in Ancient Rome and the American way of life. With court cases, such as The Scopes Trial in the United States in the 1920's, Darwin's ideas and theories were abolished from the schools and were considered unworthy of teaching in the institutional form.

Types of societal evolution could be classified as The Great Depression of the 1930's, the terrorist attacks on September 11th, 2001, the Vietnam War, the Counter-Culture Revolution of 1968, WWI and WWII, The start of space exploration, The expansion of the U.S. Constitution, the Cuban Missile Crises, The Reagan Presidency and Watergate. All these examples had a profound effect on the evolution of United States and the world's history. Darwinism and the theory of survival of the fittest can be seen embodied in these societal changes. Survival of fittest is the battle of two opposing sides for supreme power over one's land, money or territory. Good examples of this would be wars, protests, strikes and civil war. The stronger of the two people, animals, countries, governments, economies, etc.... would survive and the weaker will be overthrown or taken over. A perfect example of this would be the recent war in Iraq. The more powerful American and coalition forces invaded Iraq and overthrew the tyrannical government of Saddam Hussein. That is a perfect example of the theory of survival of fittest instituted by Darwin in the Victorian Era.

7.6: The Conclusion

In Conclusion, we can see that societal evolution and literary evolution are vastly different in explanation. We can also see how both types of evolution deals with some aspect of Darwinian thinking. Societal is more factual and literary is more fictional. Secondly, we can also see the evolution of writing styles in the Victorian Era and different ways of one's expression. Thirdly, we can see the evolution of character not only in regards to environment, but also in regards to personality as well in both literary and societal evolution.

The Conclusions

The Decline and fall of the Roman Empire and the Echoes it has toward America's future.

Including commentaries from Edward Gibbon and Peter Bender

"Pyrrhus, when his friends congratulated to him his victory over the Romans under Fabricius, but with great slaughter of his own side, said to them, "Yes; but if we have such another victory, we are undone."
Francis Bacon
Apothegms. No. 193

Conclusion
By Peter Bender

Another good source to look at for a conclusion to this thesis would be the article written by Peter Bender called, "America the New Roman Empire?" In this article, found in Orbis, a journal on world affairs, talks about the echoes of the Roman Empire seen in American society and politics. This article discusses society, politics, economics and geography as a comparison between the two superpowers. Geography, which was discussed in chapter 1 of this thesis, is seen as one of the main focal points of comparison between the two empires.

Bender states, in his article, about wars, "The second great similarity between Americans and Romans is linked to the question of why both decided not to remain on their "islands" but instead deeply engage themselves, politically and militarily, beyond the protective seas."[197] This question brings an interesting conclusion. Why did they inflict their strength and power beyond their border? Well, to become a superpower you must have good leaders, a strong economy, a strong social structure and society base and extensive amount of land. The only difference between the Americans and Romans was that the Romans gained their land by force and war. The Americans used their minds and money to purchase land in the union to expand the empire. According to Bender, the answer is:

"The oceans ceased to offer protection. The Romans concluded this during the First Punic War, which they were dragged into by carelessly

responding to a dubious request for aid from Messina in Sicily... This led to the occupation of Sicily, Sardinia and Corsica, all in an attempt to rid the Carthaginian navy of its operating bases... Within a decade, however, the enemy was trying To build a new base in southern Spain...Carthaginian general Hasdrubal was asked not to Venture any farther north than the Ebro River...When his successor, Hannibal, tried to conquer Northern Spain, Rome declared war conquering Spain's east coast[198"]

This quote explains why the Romans expanded to the south and west of its empire. It was basically a method of expansion and militaristic strategy. They wanted to keep the Carthaginians from expanding their empire into Europe. In order to stop them from expanding, Bender states, "The Romans had to conquer all these lands to keep them from going under the rule of the Carthaginians." [199] According to Bender, other things Rome had to endure during this time of expansion were the eloquent Greeks from Pergamon and Rhodes, the Antiochos of Syria and the Syrian king. Expansion into these areas of the world as well, granted Rome protection from outsiders and barbarian groups such as the Huns, Goths, Ottomans of the Middle East and Carthaginians of Northern Africa.

Bender states, that the United States is similar to the Romans in this case, in examining World War II and the League of Nations, later to become the United Nations. With the start of the League of Nations under Woodrow Wilson in 1916, America and other countries in the region of Germany gained control through this organization of nations.

After World War I, I the United Nations served the same purpose, to police and protect world cultures, values and customs. The League of Nations, in comparison to the Roman expansion, served the same purpose. The United States expanded through organizations while the Romans expanded through war and force. The League of Nations and NATO were formed as a protective measure to make sure Adolf Hitler, the leader of the New European elite, couldn't expand his empire outside those countries he already did conquer.

One other similarity between the Americans and the Romans is on the fact of world power and world domination. Bender states, "Rome's and America's power increased slowly and steadily until each grew into a superpower that could no longer be resisted and was seen by many as a salvation." [200] He also states, " Restricting itself to the "island" appeared to be less and less practical, yet only extraordinary challenges led to be less and less protective seas; and only existential threats, real or imagined, would lead to long-term commitments in other countries and on other continents."[201] Bender is basically stating that both America and Rome were seen as the superpowers and as the superpowers expanded they were looked upon for help by the smaller surrounding countries. They were looked at as "Police States;" countries that would police the world and spread their ideas through this policing. According to Bender, "Rome and America both expanded in order to achieve security…The Romans and Americans both eventually found themselves in a geographical and political position that they not originally desired, but which they then gladly accepted and firmly maintained." [202] This last quote of Bender about acceptance and maintenance talked about their statuses in the world and that of course was the whole idea of being the "Police State" of the world.

    Bender concludes, stating about Rome and America, "Do the parallels between the United States and Rome end here, or will they continue in an even more dramatic way? Rome ruled by forging the world of the time, into one single state; America rules indirectly steering the world with as much soft power as possible and as much hard power as necessary."[203] Also stated by Bender, "The Romans were able to rule their geographically limited world. The Americans have to deal with the entire globe: in some areas they have the say and in other they must exert their influence."[204] These quotes look at how times in the world have changed and how much more the Americans must do to hold on to their empire. The Romans ruled their civilization with ease in ancient times because of fewer competitions from outsiders and enemies, due to the lack of support and effort put forth by these other civilizations against the Roman powerhouse. The United States, on the other hand, has to contend with the whole world and all of its many countries and continents. Both had to police the world, but America has a lot more to police than Rome did. Rome did not have places like Vietnam and Iraq to contend with. Therefore, America's job is that much harder than that of Rome.

Finally, Bender leaves us with this final quote from Henry Kissinger about the state of the world:

"The road to empire leads to domestic decay because, in time, the claims of omnipotence erode domestic restraints. No empire has avoided the road to Caesarianism unless, like the British Empire, it devolved its power before this process could develop. In long-lasting empires, every problem turns into a domestic issue because the outside world no longer provides a counterweight... A deliberate quest for hegemony is the surest way to destroy the value that made The United States Great."[205]

Kissinger claims that in order to destroy the internal empire of the United States of America, countries have to get together, combine strengths and take over the country through hegemonic means. Some countries today that can be seen as threats to the United States are the European Union and China. Both are gathering strength in the important areas including economics, politics and social dynamics. Look out for that in the future, China or the European Union to contends with the United States for the role of superpower of the world.

Conclusion
By Edward Gibbon

To better understand the decline and fall of the Roman Empire, we must look at some of the historians and authors that wrote books and novels on the topic. One of the most well-known writers who wrote about the decline and fall of the Roman Empire was Edward Gibbon. He wrote a series of books called "The Decline and fall of the Roman Empire." These books discuss about Gibbon's ideas and opinions on why the Roman Empire fell.

In the critical forward, written by Hans-Friedrich Mueller, "Edward Gibbon repeatedly calls "Fanatics" all those whose deeply held religious convictions form the basis of their actions."[206] Mueller also states, "The history of religion is for Gibbon intimately connected to the decline and fall of the Roman Empire, but religion is hardly his only theme."[207] One of the major themes for the decline of the Roman Empire in Gibbon's book is that of the beginning of Christianity during the time of Constantine. According to Gibbon, the Christian religion spread across the Roman Empire because of five reasons. Gibbons book states:

"I. The inflexible but purified from narrow and unsocial spirit which had deterred the Gentiles from embracing the law of Moses; II. The doctrine of a future life, improved by every additional circumstance which could give weight and efficacy to that important truth; III. The miraculous powers ascribed to the primitive church; IV. The pure and austere morals of the

Christians; V. The union and discipline of the Christian republic, which gradually formed an independent and increasing state in the Roman Empire."[208]

Basically, we can see that the Christian religion was the secondary religion in the country, but as it grew throughout the empire it became the primary religion, leading to a split in the society during the time of Constantine. This split was disastrous, for the empire lead to the separation of church and state. According to Mueller's critical forward, Gibbon also discusses other reasons for the fall. Mueller states, "We encounter also "Barbarians," mercenary militarism, oppressive taxes, corrupt politicians, tyrannical governments and endless warfare against the enemies of the Roman order, both at home and abroad."[209] Being all underlying causes of the decline and fall, Gibbon discusses it all in a chronological order, which makes the reader understand the steps the empire took to its demise. Also according to Mueller, "Throughout the work, Gibbon does more than simply tell good stories. He looks for explanations and he looks for those explanations in institutions (Government, military and law), ethnography (The customs of people), economics (Gibbon is endlessly fascinated with trade, agricultural and arts), Geography and the heart."[210] His use of the different institutions gives him more basis to understanding the decline and fall of the Roman Empire.

Gibbon's conclusion is quite interesting, tying in all reasons for the decline and fall of the Roman Empire. The conclusion states numerous events that had an effect on the decline. The conclusion is also noted in chronological order and gives you a sense of why this actually happened to the empire. Gibbon mentions in his conclusion, 1) the artful policy of the twelve Caesars, who long maintained the name and image of free republic; 2) the disorders of military despotism; 3) the rise, establishment and sects of Christianity; 4) the foundation of Constantinople; 5) the division of monarchy; 6) the invasion and settlement of the barbarians and 7) the institutions of the civil law.[211] These were just some of the reasons, according to Gibbon, why the Roman Empire fell. The main reasons for its downfall being the rise of Christianity and formation of Constantinople, which led to the division in monarchy and a division within the government. A free republic under the twelve Caesars led to mass confusion and internal riots. The barbarians saw the empire weakening and they took advantage, to get their land back from the Romans. The barbarians attacked key military strongpoints and key military areas within the country.

Conclusion
By Joseph Aquilino

Both Bender and Gibbon discuss the downfall of the Roman Empire. Both have different outlooks on why it fell. Gibbon discusses the rise of Christianity and the economy as major issues and Bender discusses the more political and geographical issues of the empire. Gibbon, being that he was writing in 1700's, had a better perception of why the Roman Empire fell. He even goes back to discuss how and why the Holy Roman Empire of Charlemagne fell. Because of his life experiences, I would prefer Gibbon's thoughts more than I would read Bender's. Bender, being a columnist and journal writer, gave Rome a different perspective and compared Rome to the superpower of today, the United States. In looking for comparisons between both the Rome and America, I would read Bender. Bender based most of his knowledge on the American experience. Both writers had two different premises. The Gibbon premise was to discuss how and why the "Light of the World" fell into ruin in 479AD. The premise of Bender was to compare both Rome and America politically, economically and socially to see how America mirrors the path of the Roman Empire. Both authors had different writing styles-Gibbon having a more historical and chronological writing style and Bender having a more theoretic and futuristic type of writing style. The question Bender has is: Will America fall just like Rome did in 479 AD?

In my conclusion, I would like to discuss the same topics and explore the path of the United States a little bit more. As we look at the Roman Empire, what do we see? The Roman Empire demanded greatness, glory, prestige and honor. Americans learned about that greatness of Rome in their educational system, but did they ever learn about the bad rulers, riots, corruption, death, torture, taxes, self-righteousness, war-like personalities, etc. of the Roman people? The answer to that question is no. Unfortunately, Americans see the glory and light of Rome. They never saw the evil side of the empire. Why is that? Well, if you think about it, America is an empire itself. If you also think about it, you can see everything you see in Rome in America. In America there is corruption, bad presidents, high taxes, outside wars and the same selfish behaviors you saw in the Roman Empire. There were turning points in the history of both empires. The turning points came with the two greatest leaders read about and learned about in world history. Those two people I am referring to is Marcus Aurelius, the great philosopher and ruler of Rome and Abraham Lincoln, the greatest president of the United States, who saved the union from a certain peril. Why these two leaders? Well, for one both were philosophers in their own times. Both were noted for their greatness. Lincoln was noted for freeing the slaves and Marcus Aurelius was noted for being a philosopher king. Marcus Aurelius wrote the book, "The Meditations," as a biography of life and death. Marcus Aurelius was dying at that point and as you read through the book you can tell. In Aurelius' book he states as an example of his dying words, "Just that you do the right thing. The rest doesn't matter. Cold or Warm. Tired or well rested. Despised or Honored. Dying…or busy with other assignments. Because dying, too, is one of assignments in life. There well: 'to do what needs doing'."[212] What does this mean? Well, Marcus Aurelius spoke in metaphors and examples. This quote basically means that death is a part of life, but before you die you must do the work set out for you to do on earth.

Rome and United States have a lot in common with one another, as we found out from reading Bender. However, there are some things, I felt, that Bender did not touch upon. One thing Bender did not look at was the social structures of the two superpowers. Social structure, being one of the most important things that holds an empire together was not discussed. Social structure in Rome was split up into two sects, the patricians (the rich) and the plebeians (the poor). Back in the time of the Roman Empire, there were only two sects of the economy. The rich dominated the poor. In today's culture there are three sects of the economy, the rich, the poor and the working class (the middle class). The middle class make up a huge portion of America's population. The population of middle class workers in America is more than half. There is such a huge contrast in America especially with the ratio of rich to poor. There are far fewer rich people than poor people in America, but the rich have all the prestige, power and honor. Rome never used the terminology of middle class, even though an abundance of the Rome's population was working class. The rich usually ruled Rome. The poor were used as entertainment at times for the Romans. The poor were forced to be gladiators and they were sold as slaves of the state.

Another important topic, not touched on by Bender, was the economics of both Rome and America. Rome was a free state under the Caesars, with their own currency, whereas the Americans also operated in a state of freedom, with their own currency. The American ideal is capitalism. Rome's economics was based on transportation, trade, farming, the working class jobs and the Roman entertainment. Capitalism is a free market economy, which runs by free enterprise and stock markets. Economy is another major issue of downfall. We can see this in both Rome and the United States. Rome's economy declined in the later stages of its existence because of lack of work, high unemployment, bad leadership, confusion in the government, corruption and a deviant society. All these factors led to the downfall of the Roman republic. Americans, on the other hand, had many economic problems in the 1900's, with the 1929 Stock Market Crash, 1930-1940 Great Depression, period of stagflation and high unemployment in the 1960's and 1970's, high oil prices in the late 1970's, high unemployment and recession at the end of the 1980's and unemployment and staggering markets after September 11,2001. Is there a way to fix this dying economy? Yes, but that is up to the leadership of the country. In my opinion, creation of jobs and a better work ethic is what we need to better this economy. With the self-righteous, selfish attitudes of some in this country, America may continue to falter economically. The attitude of the country has been selfish and self-righteous, not caring about anyone else but yourself. If this continues, it could prove disastrous for this economy. Capitalism was made to be a free market economy, not a self-righteous and selfish one. Communism is more of a self-righteous and selfish economy. Rome and America have similar economies. Both existed through corrupt leaderships and confused societies. The last savior of Rome, Constantine, could not save the economy for Rome. The leaders after him were weak, which resulted in a weak, staggering economy. Rome's armies weakened because of the lack of money. Outsiders took advantage after economy collapsed and attacked the weakened Roman armies and Roman government.

The major question of most historians today is: What made Rome fall and did Rome have a chance to save itself? Well, I have concluded that Rome could have saved itself from its demise. There are three things the Romans did not do during the decline that proved to be perilous for the empire. Firstly, Rome's leaders did not have control of the empire and it was spinning out of control. The leaders of Rome were weak and it was up to the people of Rome to change the leadership and put good strong leaders in power. However, because of the hard economic times the people were confused on what to do with their money and they were not concentrating on government and leaders. The leaders after Constantine were poor and had limited leadership abilities. Leadership could have been fixed if the people of the country were not concerned with the economy.

Secondly, Rome could have enhanced the environment and social structure of the empire. As Rome declined, the environment and social structure declined with it. The introduction of new institutions to teach the young would have helped the empire. The introduction of churches and more schools to teach the youngsters of Rome would have helped develop a better core leadership. The spread of Christianity started a new institution in the Roman Empire called the church, but the church wasn't as powerful during the empire as it was during the Holy Roman Empire. The power of the pope came into being, during the Holy Roman Empire. Rome could have bettered its social structure if it was one of the main focuses. The environment of Rome during the decline was really bad considering they did not have adequate transportation and a place to put their garbage. Sanitation was an entity, but it was non-existent because of lack of transportation. The roads were filled with garbage. The environment of Rome was affected. The beauty of Rome became a garbage zone. People did not care about their empire anymore and they continued to ruin the environment where they lived. Ways they could have fixed this problem are few but effective. The developing of new methods of cleaning the environment would have helped. New methods of transportation for cleaning purposes should have been invented and an environment position inside the government should have been administered. Other ways of saving the environment would have been stricter laws and regulations against the people of Rome and the education of the youngsters of Rome in school about cleaning the environment.

Finally, Rome did not have an adequate facility to govern the nation from. It was susceptible to attack by the outsiders. In the early times of the Roman Empire the hills protected the government from outside aggression. As time went on the barriers and borders did not prove adequate enough for the protection of the rulers and government officials. It was susceptible to attack. Should the Romans have thought of different methods to protect their government? Yes, they should have, because it would have proved important to the well-being of the empire. What could they have done? Well, they could have built a wall around the governmental buildings to protect them from attack, mirroring that of the Ancient City of Troy. It would have been hard to attack the government. It would have given Rome a chance to rebuild the civilization. However, the Romans did not protect its government and many groups converged upon it and destroyed its beauty and honor. The leaders after Constantine, were so weak, they did not even look into methods of protection for one another and for the governmental center.

There are three things the Romans could have done to save their empire, but instead Rome fell into ruin in 479 AD because of lack of leadership, army strength and lack of social dominance. The final question you must ask yourself is: Is America following the same path as

Rome? As you know, this is not past history yet, so this is an idea or a theory. America, as strong and powerful as it is, will not be the only superpower in the world soon. In my opinion, in the next five to ten years, four new powers will emerge in the eastern hemisphere. These countries will emerge because of strong work ethic, powerful economies, good leadership and societal balance. These four countries will most likely be: China, Japan, India and the European Union. Three overpopulated nations and one a series of countries putting their resources together to build another European Empire. China, Japan and India as it stands at the moment have three of most powerful economies in Asia. With the strong work ethics, building up of defense programs and good leadership these overpopulated countries will emerge as superpowers in the future. The European Union, on the other hand, is trying to become another United States. These are several European countries coming together to create a unified front. This will probably be the second of the world powers in the next five years, with countries still joining and the economy still growing.

    America will still be a power, but its powers will diminish and four other countries in the world will match its superpower status. Just like Constantine, America had a last great savior that was killed in cold blood in 1963. John F. Kennedy tried to shape this nation for the future with various programs such as the start of the Space Program. It was a time of innovation and a time of change in America. After his death in 1963, Lyndon Baines Johnson tried to continue the programs set forth by John F Kennedy. Lyndon B Johnson's program "The Great Society" was a program to help the poor people of the country. The only good things to come out of this program were the ideas of Medicare and Medicaid. The program failed after Richard Nixon was elected president. In 1968, the United States saw its first drastic change in society since the Civil War. The counter cultural revolution sparked riots, protests and wars all over the world and in this country. The Vietnam War sparked a lot of these riots and protests in America. During this period of time people fought against the government. People did not approve of the government and its presidents. Richard Nixon was the first president to resign because of the Watergate Scandal. Periods of stagflation and high oil prices hurt the economy. This societal change in America was never solved, and to this day, never dealt with. In my opinion, America is too free the way it is now. Some restrictions must be put on Americans. The Constitution is being walked on and the work ethic of the country is nearly non-existent. These societal changes have not changed since 1963 and the question is: will they change? With a diminishing economic pattern because of 9/11/01, societal changes and weak leadership America is falling from superpower status. Will what happened to the Soviet Union happen to the United States? In my opinion, a major break up could occur, but I doubt it will get to that point. The democratic ideal will always thrive over the socialistic and communistic ideals. Will the United States fall like the Roman Empire did? Yes, it is possible, but again I doubt it will get to that point. I do think its diminished internal power will cause it to lose superpower status but as for falling into history like the Roman Empire, I do not feel that this will occur as of this lifetime.

It was scarcely possible that the eyes of contemporaries should discover in the public felicity, the latent causes of decay and corruption. This long peace, and the uniform government of the Romans, introduced a slow and secret poison into the vitals of the empire. The minds of men were gradually reduced to the same level, the fire of genius was extinguished, and even the military spirit evaporated. The natives of Europe were brave and robust. Spain, Gaul, Britain, and Illyricum, supplied the legions with excellent soldiers, and constituted the real strength of the monarchy. Their personal valour remained, but they no longer possessed that public courage which is nourished by the love of independence, the sense of national honor, the presence of danger, and the habit of command. They received laws and governors from the will of their sovereign, and trusted, for their defense, to a mercenary army. The posterity of their boldest leaders was contented with the rank of citizens and subjects. The most aspiring spirits resorted to the court or standard of the emperors; and the deserted provinces, deprived of political strength or union, insensibly sunk into the languid indifference of private life.

Appendix I

Quotes from the Great Marcus Aurelius
From his book "The Meditations"

"Begin the morning by saying to thyself, I shall meet with the busy-body, the ungrateful, arrogant, deceitful, envious, unsocial. All these things happen to them by reason of their ignorance of what is good and evil. But I who have seen the nature of the good that it is beautiful, and of the bad that it is ugly, and the nature of him who does wrong, that it is akin to me, not only of the same blood or seed, but that it participates in the same intelligence and the same portion of the divinity, I can neither be injured by any of them, for no one can fix on me what is ugly, nor can I be angry with my kinsman, nor hate him, For we are made for co-operation, like feet, like hands, like eyelids, like the rows of the upper and lower teeth. To act against one another then is contrary to nature; and it is acting against one another to be vexed and to turn away."

"Remember how long thou hast been putting off these things, and how often thou hast received an opportunity from the gods, and yet dost not use it. Thou must now at last perceive of what universe thou art a part, and of what administrator of the universe thy existence is an efflux, and that a limit of time is fixed for thee, which if thou dost not use for clearing away the clouds from thy mind, it will go and thou wilt go, and it will never return."

"...Why should a man have any apprehension about the change and dissolution of all the elements? For it is according to nature, and nothing is evil which is according to nature."

"They know not how many things are signified by the words stealing, sowing, buying, keeping quiet, seeing what ought to be done; for this is not affected by the eyes, but by another kind of vision."

"If thou workest at that which is before thee, following right reason seriously, vigorously, calmly, without allowing anything else to distract thee, but keeping thy divine part pure, as if thou shouldst be bound to give it back immediately; if thou holdest to this, expecting nothing, fearing nothing, but satisfied with thy present activity according to nature, and with heroic truth in every word and sound which thou utterest, thou wilt live happy. And there is no man who is able to prevent this."

"Take away thy opinion, and then there is taken away the complaint, 'I have been harmed.' Take away the complaint, 'I have been harmed,' and the harm is taken away."

"Do not act as if thou wert going to live ten thousand years. Death hangs over thee. While thou livest, while it is in thy power, be good."

"How much trouble he avoids who does not look to see what his neighbour says or does or thinks, but only to what he does himself, that it may be just and pure."

"Be like the promontory against which the waves continually break, but it stands firm and tames the fury of the water around it."

"Everything harmonizes with me, which is harmonious to thee, O Universe. Nothing for me is too early nor too late, which is in due time for thee. Everything is fruit to me which thy seasons bring, O Nature: from thee are all things, in thee are all things, to thee all things return."

"Remember too on every occasion which leads thee to vexation to apply this principle: not that this is a misfortune, but that to bear it nobly is good fortune."

"Things themselves touch not the soul, not in the least degree; nor have they admission to the soul, nor can they turn or move the soul: but the soul turns and moves itself alone, and whatever judgements it may think proper to make, such it makes for itself the things which present themselves to it."

"If this is neither my own badness, nor an effect of my own badness, and the common weal is not injured, why am I troubled about it? And what is the harm to the common weal?"

"Every soul, the philosopher says, is involuntarily deprived of truth; consequently in the same way it is deprived of justice and temperance and benevolence and everything of the kind. It is most necessary to bear this constantly in mind, for thus thou wilt be more gentle towards all."

"The perfection of moral character consists in this, in passing every day as the last, and in being neither violently excited nor torpid nor playing the hypocrite."

"The best way of avenging thyself is not to become like the wrong doer."

"Thou sufferest this justly: for thou choosest rather to become good to-morrow than to be good to-day."

"Receive wealth or prosperity without arrogance; and be ready to let it go."

"Neither in thy actions be sluggish nor in thy conversation without method, nor wandering in thy thoughts, nor let there be in thy soul inward contention nor external effusion, nor in life be so busy as to have no leisure."

"In one way an arrow moves, in another way the mind. The mind indeed, both when it exercises caution and when it is employed about inquiry, moves straight onward not the less, and to its object."

"How many after being celebrated by fame have been given up to oblivion; and how many who have celebrated the fame of others have long been dead."

"It is a ridiculous thing for a man not to fly from his own badness, which is indeed possible, but to fly from other men's badness, which is impossible."

"All things are the same, familiar in experience, and ephemeral in time, and worthless in the matter. Everything now is just as it was in the time of those whom we have buried."

"Enough of this wretched life and murmuring and apish tricks. Why art thou disturbed? What is there new in this? What unsettles thee? Is it the form of the thing? Look at it. Or is it the matter? Look at it. But besides these there is nothing. Towards the gods, then, now become at last more simple and better. It is the same whether we examine these things for a hundred years or three."

"No longer talk at all about the kind of man that a good man ought to be, but be such."

"If any man has done wrong, the harm is his own. But perhaps he has not done wrong."

"Wilt thou, then, my soul, never be good and simple and one and naked, more manifest than the body which surrounds thee? Wilt thou never enjoy an affectionate and contented disposition? Wilt thou never be full and without a want of any kind, longing for nothing more, nor desiring anything, either animate or inanimate, for the enjoyment of pleasures? Nor yet desiring time wherein thou shalt have longer enjoyment, or place, or pleasant climate, or society of men with whom thou mayest live in harmony? But wilt thou be satisfied with thy present condition, and pleased with all that is about thee, and wilt thou convince thyself that thou hast everything and that it comes from the gods, that everything is well for thee, and will be well whatever shall please them, and whatever they shall give for the conservation of the perfect living being, the good and just and beautiful, which generates and holds together all things, and contains and embraces all things which are dissolved for the production of other like things? Wilt thou never be such that thou shalt so dwell in community with gods and men as neither to find fault with them at all, nor to be condemned by them?"

"Men despise one another and flatter one another; and men wish to raise themselves above one another, and crouch before one another."

"Severally on the occasion of everything that thou doest, pause and ask thyself, if death is a dreadful thing because it deprives thee of this."

"The healthy eye ought to see all visible things and not to say, I wish for green things; for this is the condition of a diseased eye."

"Have I done something for the general interest? Well then I have had my reward. Let this always be present to thy mind, and never stop doing such good."

"Think of the country mouse and of the town mouse, and of the alarm and trepidation of the town mouse."

"If it is not right, do not do it: if it is not true, do not say it. For let thy efforts be."

"Consider when thou art much vexed or grieved, that man's life is only a moment, and after a short time we are all laid out dead."

"Neither in writing nor in reading wilt thou be able to lay down rules for others before thou shalt have first learned to obey rules thyself."

"Does the light of the lamp shine without losing its splendour until it is extinguished; and shall the truth which is in thee and justice and temperance be extinguished before thy death?"```

Source Information:
www.roman-empire.net
Quotations from Marcus Aurelius

Appendix II

Map of the Roman Empire

Appendix III
Family Tree of the Early Roman Empire
"The Twelve Caesars"

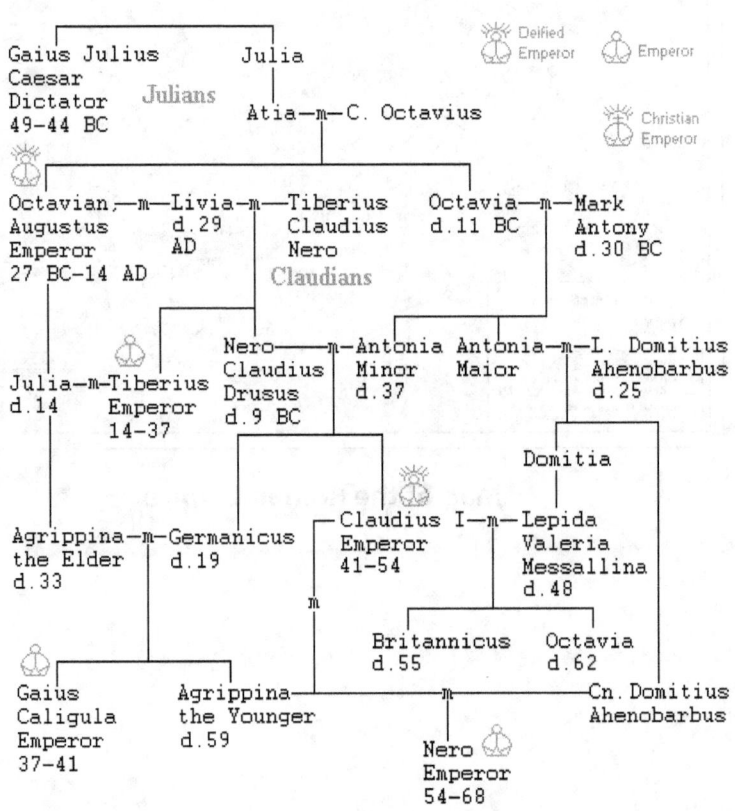

265

Appendix IV
Family tree of Flavian Emperors in Rome
"The High Point of Rome"

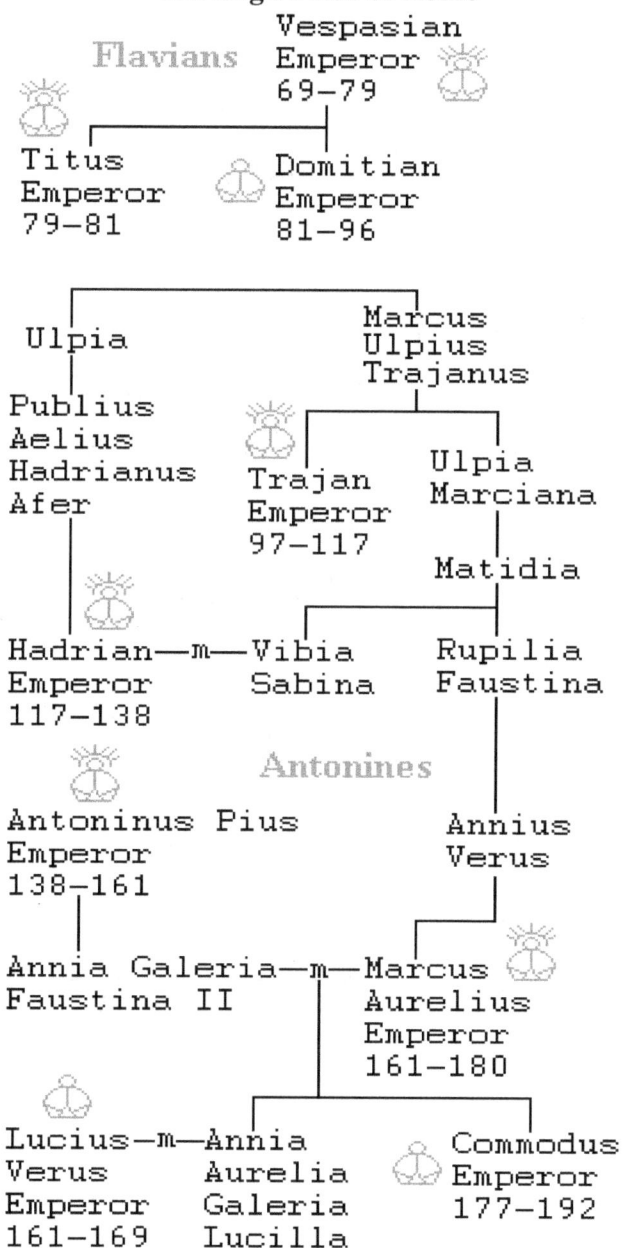

Appendix V
The Family Tree of Constantians
"The Final Saviors of Rome"

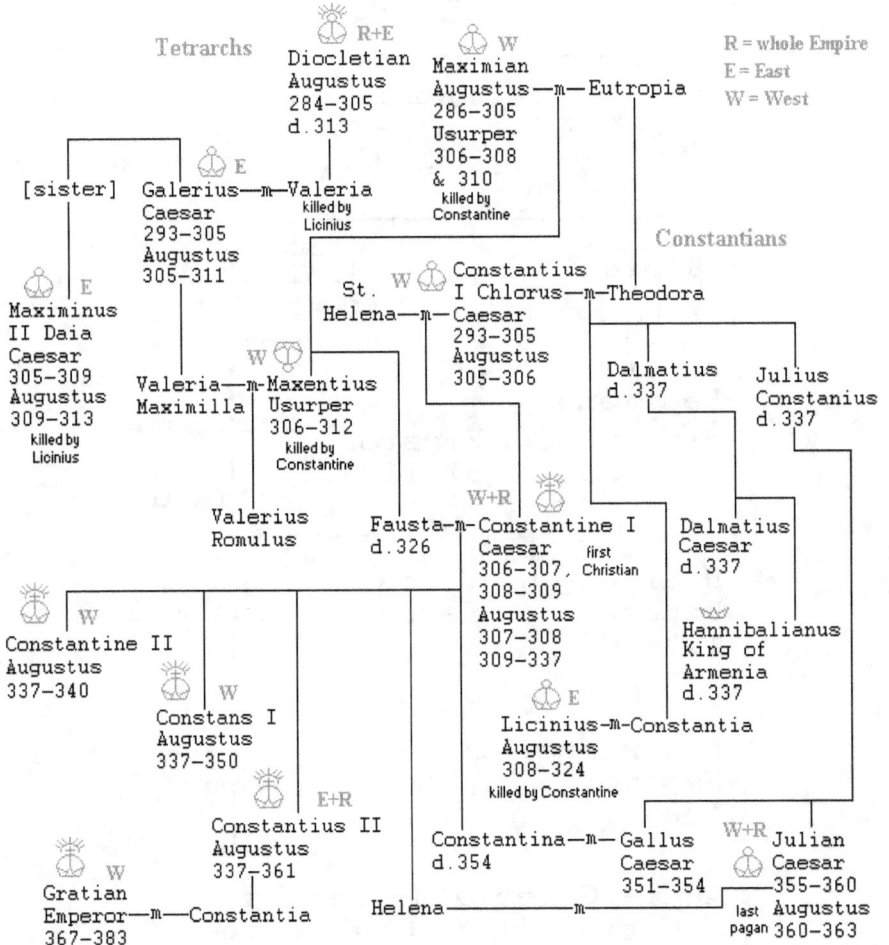

Main Sources

- Adkins, Lesley, and Roy A. Adkins. Handbook to Life in Ancient Rome. New York: Oxford University Press Inc., 1994.
- Appleman, Philip. Darwin, 3rd Edition. USA: W.W. Norton & Company Inc., 2001.
- Bender, Peter. "America: The New Roman Empire." Orbis: A Journal of World Affairs, Volume 47, Number 1, Winter 2003, pp. 145-159.
- Bartlett, Bruce. "How Excessive Government killed Ancient Rome," CATO Journal, 02733072, Fall 1994, Vol. 14, Issue 2.
- Bartlett, John. Quotations, http://www.bartleby.com, 2004.
- Boatwright, Mary T., Daniel J. Gargola, Richard J. A. Talbert. The Romans from Village to Empire: A History of Ancient Rome from the Earliest Times to Constantine. New York: Oxford University Press Inc., 2004.
- Bondanella, Peter, and Mark Musa. The Portable Machiavelli. London, England: Penguin Books Inc., 1979. Original Publication by Niccolo Machiavelli in 1469-1527.
- Borenstein, David. Quotations, http://www.quoteland.com, 1999 – 2001.
- Browning, Elizabeth. Aurora Leigh, 1992 (reprinted)
- Camus, Albert. Caligula and 3 Other Plays. New York: Vintage Books, A Division of Random House, 1958. Reprinted by Alfred A. Knopf, Inc. Translated from French version in 1944 by Stuart Gilbert.
- Carcopino, Jerome. Daily Life in Ancient Rome. Clinton, Mass., USA: Yale University Press Inc., 1960. First published in 1940.
- Carazzi, Franco. The Roman Empire, http://www.roman-empire.net, 2004.
- Christ, Karl. The Romans. Berkeley and Los Angeles, California, USA: University of California Press Inc., 1984
- Connolly, Peter, and Hazel Dodge. The Ancient City, Life in Classical Athens and Rome. United Kingdom: Oxford University Press, 1998.

- Constable, Nick. Historical Atlas of Ancient Rome. New York: Thalamus Publishing, 2003.
- Cowell, F.R. Life in Ancient Rome. New York: Berkley Publishing Group, a division of Penguin Books Inc., 1980. First published in 1961.
- Donno, Daniel. Niccolo Machiavelli "The Prince." New York: Bantam Books, A division of Random House, January 2003. First Printed in 1513 by Niccolo Machiavelli.
- Edwards, Catherine. Suetonius' Lives of the Caesars. New York: Oxford University Press Inc., 2000.
- Eliot, George. Middlemarch, 1986.
- Fink, Carole, Philipp Gassert and Detlef Junker. 1968: The World Transformed. Washington D.C., USA: The German Historical Institute, 1998
- Floyd, Chris. "What did the Romans Ever Do For us," The Ecologist, Vol. 32, No. 3, April 2002, p. 45.
- Gibbon, Edward. The History of the Decline and fall of The Roman Empire. London, England: Penguin Books Inc., 2000. First full edition published in 1776, 1781 and 1788.
- Gibbon, Edward. The History of the Decline and fall of the Roman Empire, Volume 1. London, England: Penguin Books Inc., 1995. First published in 1776 and 1781 and edited by David Womersley.
- Gibbon, Edward. Critical forward by Mueller, Hans Friedrich. The Decline and fall of the Roman Empire. New York: Random House, Inc., 2003.
- Gladiator The Movie, DVD, Directed by Ridley Scott. 2000, Universal City, California, DreamWorks LLC, starring Russell Crowe and Joaquin Phoenix.
- Grant, Michael. The Ancient Historians. Barnes & Noble Inc.: 1994. First published in 1970 by Michael Grant Publications, Ltd.
- Grant, Michael. Sick Caesars. USA: Barnes & Noble Inc., 2000. Published in the same year by Michael Grant Publications, Ltd.

- Grant, Michael. The Roman Emperors: A Biographical Guide to the Rulers of Imperial Rome 31 BC- AD 476. USA: Barnes & Noble Inc., 1997. First published in 1985 by Michael Grant Publications, Ltd.
- Grant, Michael. The Twelve Caesars. USA: Barnes & Noble Inc., 1996. First published in 1975 by Michael Grant Publications, Ltd.
- Griffen, Jasper, John Boardman and Oswyn Murray. The Oxford History of the Roman World. New York: Oxford University Press Inc., 2001. First published in 1991 as a paperback.
- Hays, Gregory. Marcus Aurelius' "The Meditations." New York: The Modern Library, A Division of Random House, 2002.
- Holland, Tom. "What Bush can learn from the Romans," The Newstateman Magazine, August 25, 2003, pp. 20-21.
- Kestler, Justin. "The Aeneid" by Virgil. New York: Spark Publishing LLC, 2002.
- Kestler, Justin. "The Prince" by Niccolo Machiavelli. New York: Spark Publishing LLC, 2002.
- Keys, David. "How Rome Polluted the World," www.geographical.co.uk, December 2003 edition, pp. 45-48
- Kissinger, Henry. Does America Need a Foreign Policy? 2001, pp. 287-288.
- Knight, Kevin. The Roman Geography, http://www.newadvent.org, 2004, also known as the Catholic Online Encyclopedia.
- Lee, Desmond. "The Republic" by Plato, 2nd Edition. London, England: Penguin Books Inc., 2003.
- Livy. Translated by Aubrey De Selincourt. The Early History of Rome. London, England: Penguin Books Inc., 2002.
- Mandelbaum, Allen. The Aeneid of Virgil. New York: Bantam Books, A division of Random House, October 1981.
- Mannix, Daniel P. The Way of the Gladiator. New York: www.ibooks.com distributed by Simon and Schuster Inc., 2001.

- Oracle Education Foundation. The Roman Empire, http://library.thinkquest.org 1996 Also known as SPQRonline.com
- Payne, Robert. Horizon's Ancient Rome. New York: www.ibooks.com distributed by American Heritage Inc.: 2001
- Peters, Timothy. "A History of Images: Christianity and Historiography in the Later Decline and Fall of the Roman Empire. EBSCO Publishing, 2002.
- Plutarch. Translated by Rex Warner and introductions by Robin Seager. Fall of the Roman Republic: The Tale of Six Lives. London, England: Penguin Books Inc., 1972.
- Reid, Brian Holden. The American Civil War. London, England: Cassell & Co., Wellington House, 2000.
- Rizzo, John. "Surfing Roman History," Fra Noi Italian Newspaper of Chicago, April 2004 edition, Section 1A.
- Robinson, Matthew. "Roman Lessons for Prof. Gingrich," Human Events, August 4, 2000, p. 19.
- Saunders, Trevor J. "The Politics" by Aristotle. London, England: Penguin Books Inc., 1992.
- Scarre, Chris. The Penguin Historical Atlas of Ancient Rome. London, England: Penguin Books Inc., 1995.
- Scarre, Chris. Chronicle of the Roman Emperors: The Reign-by-Reign Record of the Rulers of Imperial Rome. London, England: Thames &Hudson Ltd., 1995
- Slayden, Greg. Italian Mountain Ranges, http://www.peakbagger.com, 2004, also known as the Mountain Explorer all around the world.
- Staccioli, R.A. Frommer's Rome Past & Present. Rome, Italy: Wiley Publishing Inc., 2003.
- Tacitus. Translated by Kenneth Wellesley. The Histories. London, England: Penguin Books Inc., 1995.
- The Roman Empire in the First Century, DVD, directed by Margaret Koval. 2001; PBS (Public Broadcasting Service), New York, NY: Goldfarb and Koval Production, Inc.

- Vedder, Richard. "Capital Crimes: Political Centers as Parasite Economies," USA Today Magazine, 01617389, Sept. 1997, Vol. 126, Issue 2628, pp. 20-26.
- Wales, Jimmy. The Roman Empire, http://en.wikipedia.org, 2004 also known as Wikipedia: The Free Encyclopedia.
- Walsh, Mary Dr. Thesis Paper: Machiavelli, Politics and the Public Realm, 2001.
- Webster's Dictionary, 6th Pocket Sized edition, 1996.
- Webster's Dictionary of Quotations, 1995.
- Webster's New World Dictionary, 1st Pocket sized edition, 1990.
- Wells, Colin. The Roman Empire, 2nd edition. Cambridge, Mass., USA: Harvard University Press Inc., 2002. First published in 1984.
- Woolf, Virginia. The Three Guineas, 1938.
- Wootton, David. "Narrative, Irony and Faith in Gibbon's Decline and Fall," Brunel University, 2001.
- Zimmer, Hans, and Lisa Gerrard. Gladiator The Movie Soundtrack. A Universal Music Company. CD. New York, NY. 2000.

Additional Sources of Information

- American Academy of the Child, 2004, Children and Divorce and Gays and Lesbians
- American Academy of Pediatrics, 2000, Work related stresses on Women.
- Bartlett, John, and Justin Kaplin. Bartlett's Familiar Quotations, 16th Edition. USA: Little, Brown and Company Inc., 1992.
- Beschloss, Michael. American Heritage: The Presidents, Every Leader from Washington to Bush. New York: American Heritage Inc., 2003.
- Buttle, Nicholas. "Republican Constitutionalism: A Roman Ideal," The Journal of Political Philosophy, Volume 9, Number 3, 2001, pp. 331-349.
- Copleston, Frederick S.J. A History of Philosophy, Volume 1 Greece and Rome from Socrates to Plotinus. New York: Image Books, Doubleday Inc., 1993.

- Dyck, Ludwig Heinrich. "Caesar's First Great Campaign," Military History Magazine, February 2004, pp. 50- 56
- Ehrlich, Eugene, and Marshall DeBruhl. The International Thesaurus of Quotations. New York: HarperCollins Publishers Inc., 1996.
- Elton, Hugh. "Off the Battlefield: The Civilian's View of Late Roman Soldiers," Expedition Magazine, 00144738, 1997, Vol. 39, Issue 2.
- Feldman, Louis H. "Rabbinic Insights on the Decline and Forthcoming Fall of the Roman Empire," Journal for the Study of Judaism, XXXI, 2000, Yeshiva University.
- Fines, John. Who's Who in the Middle Ages. New York: Barnes and Noble Inc., 1995.
- Goldsworthy, Adrian. Roman Warfare. London, England: Cassell & Co., Wellington House, 2000.
- Goldsworthy, Adrian. The Complete Roman Army. London, England: Thames & Hudson Ltd., 2003.
- Hildinger, Erik. Swords Against the Senate: The Rise of the Roman Army and the fall of the Republic. USA: Da Capo Press Inc., 2002.
- Johnson, Curt, and David L. Bongard. The Harper Encyclopedia of Military Biography. Edison, NJ, USA: Castle Books Inc., 1992.
- Laurence, Ray. " Metaphors, Monuments and texts: the Life course in Roman Culture," World Archaeology, Vol. 31, pp. 442-455.
- Magee, Brian. The Story of Philosophy. New York: DK Publishing Inc., 2001.
- Mangione, Jerre, and Ben Morreale. La Storia: Five Centuries of the Italian American Experience. New York: HarperCollins Publishers Inc., 1993.
- Mommsen, Theodor. The Provinces of the Roman Empire. New York: Barnes & Noble Inc., 1996.
- Nelson, Eric Ph.D. The Complete Idiot's Guide to the Roman Empire. Indianapolis, IN, USA: Penguin Group Inc., 2002.
- New Internationalist. "A Brief History of Slavery," 03059529, August 2001, Issue 337.

- Platt, Suzy. Respectfully Quoted: A Dictionary of Quotations. New York: Barnes & Noble Inc., 1993.
- Rosen, Stanley. The Philosopher's Handbook: Essential Readings from Plato to Kant. USA: Random House Inc., 2000.
- Sahakian, William Ph.D., and Mabel Lewis Sahakian. Ideas of The Great Philosophers. New York: Barnes & Noble Inc., 1996.
- Schuster, Angela M.H. "Rome 1-1000," Archaeology Magazine, 00038113, Jan/Feb 2000, Vol. 53, Issue 1.
- Slobogan, Nancy (CNN News Reporter), May 16th, 2001 Women and Work Related Stress (additional source: www.cnn.com)
- Snobelen, Stephen David. " A further Irony: Apocalyptic Readings of Edward Gibbon's Decline and Fall of the Roman Empire," Canadian journal of History, XXXIII, December 1998, pp. 387-416.
- Twiss, Miranda. The Most Evil Men and Women in History. New York: Barnes & Noble Inc., 2002
- U.S. Congress, Senate, 76th Congress, 3rd Session, Report 1615
- Viorst, Milton. The Great Documents of Western Civilization. New York: Barnes & Noble Inc., 1994.
- Wells, Peter S. The Battle That Stopped Rome. USA: W.W. Norton & Company Inc., 2003.
- Widdows, P.F. Lucan's Civil War. USA: Indiana University Press Inc., 1988.
- Williams, Stephen, and Gerard Friell. "The Survival of the Eastern Roman Empire," History Today Magazine, November 1998, pp. 40 – 46.

[1] Meaning from Webster's Dictionary (1996) p. 189 Definition of Peninsula

[2] Boatwright, Gargola and Talbert (2004) p. 1, Part 1 On the history of Italian Geography and its importance
[3] Ibid, (2004) p. 1, Part 1
[4] Ibid (2004) p.2, Part 1
[5] Ibid (2004) p.2, Part 1
[6] Ibid (2004) p.2, Part 1
[7] Ibid (2004) p.2,
[8] Adkins & Adkins (1994) p.105, Chapter 3 The Early History of Rome
[9] www.library.thinkquest.org (1999) on the geography of Rome and modern day Italy

[10] Ibid (1999) on the diversity of the land in Rome
[11] SPQR online www.Library.thinkquest.org (1999) On the defense of the Apennines Mountains against outside entities
[12] Boatwright, Gargola &Talbert (2004) p.2, Part 1 On the topography of Italy and its mountains
[13] Ibid (2004) p.1, Part 1 On the Dominance of the Apennine mountain range

[14] Catholic Encyclopedia www.newadvent.org (2003)
[15] Ibid (2003) On the center of Apennine Mountains
[16] Ibid (2003) On the highest peak of the Apennine Mountains
[17] The Mountain Explorer www.peakbagger.com (2001) On the Alps Mountains in northern Italy

[18] Ibid (2001) Highest Point of Alps

[19] www.Encyclopedia.com (2004) Economic importance of the Alps to Italy
[20] Ibid (2004) Hydroelectric Power
[21] Website: http://en.wikipedia.org/wiki/Appalachian_Mountains Wikipedia; constant updates of geography (Mar. 2004) on the Appalachian Mountain range; additional resources www.yahoo.com and www.excite.com
[22] Ibid (Mar. 2004) on the Atlantic Plains Land
[23] Ibid (Mar.2004) on the Appalachian Highlands in the Eastern United States
[24] Ibid (Mar. 2004) on The Great Plains
[25] Ibid (Mar. 2004) on the Great Plains region
[26] Ibid (Mar. 2004) on the Rocky Mountains
[27] Ibid (Mar. 2004) on the Grand Canyon

[28] Ibid (Mar. 2004) on the Area of the United States
[29] [29] New World Webster's Dictionary (1995) meaning of the "Archipelago" p. 30

[30] Website: http://en.wikipedia.org Wikipedia; constant updates of geography (Mar. 2004) on the rivers, lakes and seas of America

[31] Bender, Peter (2003) "America, The New Roman Empire?" Caption about the life of Peter Bender, p. 145
[32] Ibid (2003), p. 145
[33] Ibid (2003), p. 146
[34] Ibid (2003) p.146 Additional Resources used by Bender: U.S. Congress, Senate, 76th Congress, 3rd Session, Report 1615 (To accompany H.R. 8026), pp. 1-31
[35] Ibid (2003) p.146
[36] New World Webster's Dictionary (1995) meaning of isolationist, p. 316
[37] Columbia Encyclopedia online; sixth edition; www.bartleby.com (2001) about Pyrrhus the Molossian King against the Romans

[38] Bender, Peter (2003) "America, The New Roman Empire?" p. 146

[39] Columbia online Encyclopedia; sixth edition; www.bartleby.com (2001) about Monroe
[40] Bender, Peter (2003) "America, The New Roman Empire?" p. 146
[41] Ibid (2003) p.146
[42] Ibid (2003) p.146

[43] Ibid (2003) p.147

[44] Ibid (2003) p.147
[45] Ibid (2003) p.148

[46] Ibid (2003) p.148

[47] Ibid (2003) p.148

[48] New World Webster's Dictionary (1995) meaning of "island," p.315`
[49] Saunders, Trevor (1981) Penguin Books (I, ii) The State of the Individual p.59
Additional Resources: The International Thesaurus of Quotations by Eugene Ehrlich and Marshall DeBruhl p.518 under Politics and Politicians.
[50] Ibid (1981) Penguin Books (I, ii) The Formation of the State p. 59
[51] Ibid (1981) Penguin Books (I, ii) The State of the Individual p. 60
[52] The International Thesaurus of Quotations by Eugene Ehrlich and Marshall DeBruhl p.519 Quote from Albert Camus, *Notebooks* 1935-1942(1962), 2
[53] Webster's Dictionary of Quotations (1995) Quote from Niccolo Machiavelli, *The Prince;* Section on Leaders and Rulers p. 241
[54] Ibid (1995) Quote from Niccolo Machaivelli, *The Prince;* Section on Fear p. 142

[55] Ibid (1995) Quote from Aristotle's *The Politics;* Section on Leaders and Rulers p. 239
[56] Kestler, Justin "The Aeneid" by Virgil (2002) Character List and Evolution, p. 7

[57] Ibid (2002) Character List and Evolution, p. 7
[58] Ibid (2002) Character List and Evolution, p. 7

[59] Mandelbaum, Allen (1971) "The Aeneid" by Virgil; translated by the author, Book XII, p.335-336 about the battle between Turnus and Aeneas
[60] Kestler, Justin "The Aeneid" by Virgil (2002) Symbols, p. 22
[61] Mandelbaum, Allen (1971) "The Aeneid" by Virgil, Book IV, p. 82 about the love of Dido for Aeneas

[62] Kestler, Justin "The Aeneid" by Virgil (2002) Symbols, p. 22

[63] Ibid (2002) Symbols, p. 22
[64] Ibid (2002) Symbols, p. 22
[65] Ibid (2002) Symbols, p.22

[66] Ibid (2002) Symbols, p. 22

[67] Mandelbaum, Allen (1971) "The Aeneid" by Virgil, Book IV, p. 138 & 139 about the golden bough
[68] Ibid (1971) Book I, p. 3
[69] Kestler, Justin (2002) "The Aeneid" by Virgil, p. 23
[70] Thames &Hudson (1995) about Gaius Caesar Augustus (Caligula) biography, p. 36
[71] Ibid (1995) p. 36
[72] Ibid (1995) p. 37
[73] Ibid (1995) p. 41
[74] Hays, Gregory (2002) "The Meditations" by Marcus Aurelius; the new translation. Hays introduction, p. 1
[75] Thames & Hudson (1995) biography of Marcus Aurelius, p. 112
[76] Ibid (1995) p. 113
[77] Hays, Gregory (2002) "The Meditations" by Marcus Aurelius; the new translation, p. 134
[78] Ibid (2002) p. 102
[79] Ibid (2002) p. 102
[80] Grant, Michael (2000) "The Sick Caesars" about Caligula's mental problems, p. 34

[81] Ibid (2000) p. 42
[82] Ibid (2000) p. 42
[83] Camus, Albert (1958) "Caligula and three other plays" Focus on Caligula, p. 24
[84] Ibid (1958) p. 71
[85] Grant, Michael (2000) Focus on Caligula's mental problems, p. 43
[86] Ibid (2000) p. 64

[87] Ibid (2000) about Marcus Aurelius health problems, p. 64
[88] Hays, Gregory (2002) "The Meditations" by Marcus Aurelius, p. 19
[89] Penguin Classics "The Republic" by Plato (2003) re-print of older 1987 version of book. Part II Preliminaries, I. First Principles of Social Organization, p. 53.

[90] Ibid (2003) p. 56

[91] Ibid (2003) p. 59
[92] Penguin Classics "The Politics" by Aristotle (1992) re-print of the 1961 version of book, Book II, Part ii p. 104 Extreme Unity in Plato's Republic.

[93] Ibid (1992) p. 115

[94] Ibid (1992) p. 118
[95] Ibid (1992) p. 110
[96] Ibid (1992) IV, iv, p. 243
[97] Ibid (1992) IV, iv, p. 244
[98] Ibid (1992) IV, xi, p. 264
[99] Webster's New World Dictionary (1990) meaning of the word tyrant, p. 639
[100] Ibid (1990) meaning of tyranny, p. 639
[101] Penguin Classics "The Republic" by Plato (2003) re-print of a book from 1987, Part XI, Book VIII, p. 299

[102] Webster's New World Dictionary (1990) meaning of oligarchy, p. 411
[103] Penguin Classics "The Republic" by Plato (2003) re-print of a book from 1987, Part XI, Book VIII, p. 299

[104] Ibid (2003) p. 118
[105] [105] Donno, Daniel "The Prince" by Niccolo Machaivelli (2003) re-print of a 1981 book. The Discourses upon the First Ten Books of Titus Livy, p. 111
[106] Ibid (2003) p. 110 of the Discourses
[107] Ibid (2003) p. 111
[108] Ibid (2003) p. 111
[109] Dr. Mary Walsh. Thesis Paper: Machiavelli, Politics and the Public Realm (2001) p. 3

[110] Ibid (2001) p. 3 Additional Resources: Machaivelli p. 61

[111] Ibid (2001) p. 3
[112] Ibid (2001) p. 3
[113] Ibid (2001) p. 3
[114] Ibid (2001) p. 16
[115] Beschloss, Michael (American Heritage Magazine writer) "The Presidents" (2003) Introduction, pps 9-15 talking about the good and bad times of American history
[116] Ibid (2003) p. 10 of the Introduction

[117] Ibid (2003) p. 10 of the Introduction
[118] Ibid (2003) p. 11 of the Introduction
[119] Fink, Carole; Gassert, Philipp; Junker, Detlef "1968: The World Transformed" (1998) p. 2 of the Introduction
[120] Ibid (1998) p.2 of the Introduction
[121] Ibid (1998) p. 3 of the Introduction
[122] Ibid (1998) p. 3 of the Introduction

[123] Ibid (1998) p. 3 of the Introduction
[124] Cowell, F.R. "Life in Ancient Rome" (1980) Cowell explains the importance of the family in ancient Roman society, by looking at the Roman family in depth. Chapter III, p. 55
[125] Ibid (1980) p.56 Marcus Aurelius statement on the family and love
[126] Capital Crimes: Political Centers as Parasite Economies, By: Veddar, Richard K., USA Today Magazine, 01617389, Sep 97, Vol. 26 Issue 2628, p.1

[127] Ibid (Sept 1997) p. 1
[128] Frommer's Guide to Past and Present Roman Architecture (2003) p. 7 about the Coliseum structure and beauty
[129] Ibid (2003) p. 7 history of the building cycle of the Coliseum

[130] Ibid (2003) p. 7 building materials and size of the Coliseum building

[131] The Ancient City: Life in Classical Athens and Rome by Connolly, Peter & Dodge, Hazel (1998) p. 192 on the lifespan of the Coliseum

[132] Ibid (2003) p. 7 interior of the Coliseum
[133] Ibid (2003) p. 8 more on the interior of the Coliseum
[134] Ibid (2003) p. 10
[135] Ibid (2003) p. 13
[136] The Ancient City: Life in Classical Athens and Rome by Connolly, Peter & Dodge, Hazel (1998) p. 192 on the lifespan of the Coliseum
[137] Frommer's Guide to Past and Present Roman Architecture (2003) p. 14

[138] Ibid (2003) p. 14
[139] Ibid (2003) p. 14
[140] Ibid (2003) p. 14
[141] Ibid (2003) p. 18
[142] Ibid (2003) p. 26
[143] Ibid (2003) p. 26
[144] www.brooklyn.cuny.edu (2003) Brooklyn College professor talks about the Basilica Julia

[145] http://www.vroma.org/~forum/rostra.html (2003) Forum Romanum Website talked about the Rostra

[146] http://www.vroma.org/~forum/tcaspol.html (2003) Forum Romanum Website talking about the legend of the Temple of Castor and Pollux the twin sons of Jupiter in Greek mythology

[147] Ibid (2003) http://www.vroma.org/~forum/tcaspol.html

[148] Frommer's Guide to Past and Present Roman Architecture (2003) p. 32

[149] Ibid (2003) p. 34

[150] http://www.roman-empire.net/tours/rome/temple-vesta.html (2003) Roman Empire.net talks about the Temple of Vesta in the center of the Forum Romanus

[151] Frommer's Guide to Past and Present Roman Architecture (2003) p. 38

[152] Ibid (2003) p. 30
[153] Ibid (2003) p. 17
[154] Ibid (2003) p. 50
[155] Ibid (2003) p. 43
[156] Ibid (2003) p. 43
[157] Mannix, Daniel P. "The Way of the Gladiator" (2001) Chapter 1, p. 1 an explanation of the times in Rome during the time of Nero, which led to the start of the gladiator games at the Coliseum.

[158] Ibid (2001) Chapter I, p. 2
[159] Ibid (2001) Chapter I, p. 2
[160] Ibid (2001) Chapter I, p. 2
[161] Ibid (2001) Chapter I, p. 5

[162] Ibid (2001) Chapter XII, p. 183
[163] Ibid (2001) Chapter XIII, p. 193
[164] Ibid (2001) Chapter XIII, p. 193
[165] [165] Reid, Brain H. "The American Civil War" (1999) p. 62 Southern opposition to Northern disapproval of slavery in the south on the plantations and farms.

[166] Ibid (1999) p. 62

[167] Capital Crimes: Political Centers as Parasite Economies. By: Vedder, Richard K., USA Today Magazine, 01617389, Sep 97, Vol. 126, Issue 2628, p. 1

[168] Slobogan, Nancy (News Reporter), CNN News (May 16, 2001) on Women and Work Related Stress (found on CNN.com)

[169] American Academy of Pediatrics (2000) on work related stresses on women and on relationship.

[170] American Academy of the Child (2004) on children and divorce
[171] Ibid (2004) on gay and lesbians raising children

[172] Ibid (2004) on gay and lesbians
[173] Ibid (2004) on gay and lesbians
[174] Appleman, Philip "Darwin" (2001) pp. 3 of Part I the introduction

[175] Ibid (2001) pp. 3
[176] Ibid (2001) pp. 3
[177] Ibid (2001) pp. 3
[178] [178] Ibid (2001) pp. 4
[179] Ibid (2001) pp. 4 & 5
[180] Ibid (2001) pp. 4
[181] Ibid (2001) pp. 373
[182] Ibid (2001) pp. 373
[183] Ibid (2001) pp. 202
[184] Ibid (2001) pp. 202
[185] Ibid (2001) pp. 202
[186] Ibid (2001) pp. 200
[187] Ibid (2001) pp. 201
[188] Ibid (2001) pp. 201
[189] Ibid (2001) pp. 201
[190] Eliot, George "Middlemarch" (1986) pp. 6
[191] Ibid (1986) pp. 6
[192] Ibid (1986) pp. 8
[193] Ibid (1986) pp. 9
[194] Woolf, Virginia "The Three Guineas" (1938) pp. 100
[195] Appleman, Philip "Darwin" (2001) pp. 377
[196] Ibid (2001) pp. 377
[197] Bender, Peter "America, The New Roman Empire?" (2003) p. 148 of Orbis, A journal of World Affairs
[198] Ibid (2003) p. 148
[199] Ibid (2003) p. 148
[200] Ibid (2003) p. 150
[201] Ibid (2003) p. 151
[202] Ibid (2003) p. 151
[203] Ibid (2003) p. 158
[204] Ibid (2003) p. 158
[205] Ibid (2003) p. 158 additional sources: Henry A. Kissinger, *Does America Need a Foreign Policy?* pp. 287-288 (2001) after the 9/11/01 attacks on the Twin Towers and the Pentagon

[206] Gibbon, Edward "The Decline and Fall of the Roman Empire" Critical Forward p. XXV by Mueller, Hans-Friedrich (2003) reprint of a book made and printed in 1737 by Edward Gibbon

[207] Ibid (2003) Critical Forward p. XXVI
[208] Ibid (2003) Chapter XV by Gibbon p. 238

[209] [209] Ibid (2003) Critical Forward p. XXVI
[210] Ibid (2003) Critical forward p. XXIX
[211] Ibid (2003) Chapter LXX p. 1251 Conclusion
[212] Gregory Hays, A New Translation of Marcus Aurelius' classic "The Meditations" (2003) reprint of a book written by Marcus Aurelius in 121-180 AD p. 69 of Book 6

Sensational Publications is here to help authors!
We are a self-publishing company made to put the money back where it belongs-in the authors' hands. Sensational Publications was built by authors after seeing how little compensation other companies paid authors for their work. We deliver high quality books for a lower price, while giving you higher compensation for each book sale.
We can do everything for you, just send us your manuscript and we will make it happen. We have fast turnaround times with most books being published within 1-2 months. We have a strong list of distributors including, but not limited to: Amazon, Barnes and Noble, Baker & Taylor, Ingram and more-all included in our low price. We can also sell your book internationally.

For more information please visit: sensationalpublications.com

www.ingramcontent.com/pod-product-compliance
Lightning Source LLC
Chambersburg PA
CBHW051421290426
44109CB00016B/1385